G000165044

no guts no glory

How to build a youth ministry that lasts

Edited by
Alan Stewart

Contributors
Steve Couch
Al Horn
Ken Moser
Alan Stewart
Tim Thornborough
Edward Vaughan

No Guts No Glory
Second edition
© Matthias Media 2000
First published 1990

Matthias Media
(St Matthias Press Ltd ACN 067 558 365)
PO Box 225
Kingsford NSW 2032
Australia
Telephone: (02) 9663 1478; international: +61-2-9663-1478
Facsimile: (02) 9663 3265; international: +61-2-9663-3265
Email: info@matthiasmedia.com.au
Internet: www.matthiasmedia.com.au

Matthias Media (USA)
Telephone: 330 953 1702; international: +1-330-953-1702
Facsimile: 330 953 1712; international: +1-330-953-1712
Email: sales@matthiasmedia.com
Internet: www.matthiasmedia.com

Scripture taken from the Holy Bible, NEW INTERNATIONAL
VERSION®. Copyright © 1973, 1978, 1984 by Biblica, Inc. All rights
reserved worldwide. Used by permission.

ISBN 978 1 876326 22 7

Cover design and typesetting by Matthias Media.

Contents

Preface to the second edition

No *Guts, No Glory* was first published in 1990 when the three original authors were in their early 30s. It is now ten years on, and only one of us works directly in youth work—however, the other two have teenage children and so are doing youth work of a different kind. We are still wholeheartedly committed to the principles in this book but are the first to admit that we still have lots to learn regarding youth work, be it in a church context or as a parent. I wish to express our great gratitude to the young men and women who commit so much of their lives to caring for the teenagers of our churches, and we pray that God will bless their labours to see many of these young people brought into his kingdom.

Given the physical effects of an extra ten years, I suggested that we should perhaps change the title of this book to *A Bit of a Gut, No Glory*. I was talked out of it, not least because some of the new contributors to this new edition have yet to suffer the ravages of approaching middle-age. I am grateful for their efforts, especially those of our English brothers, Steve Couch, Al Horn and Tim Thornborough.

So ten years on, it is still *No Guts, No Glory*—meaning that in the face of opposition and the seeming weakness of the gospel, it takes courage to hold the line and call people to obedience in Christ. It's in maintaining that courage that we will see the glory of God in the face of Christ as he works in people, or as people understand the gospel and are transformed to be like him.

Alan Stewart

EDITOR
AUGUST 2000

How to use this book

No Guts, No Glory is a resource for leaders of Christian youth groups. We have put together some material to help you build a youth group that lasts–that is, a group that is committed to the Gospel of Jesus Christ and looks forward to spending eternity with him. We write from the conviction that young people can be changed as they come into contact with this Jesus in the living Word of God.

This book is designed so that it can easily be used with youth leaders. There are eleven chapters, looking at different areas of youth ministry. Included in each chapter are questions for group discussion.

You could use these chapters as the basis for youth leaders' meetings. Perhaps you could encourage your leaders to read each chapter and write answers to the questions before the meeting. Then, when you meet, you would only need to summarise the material, and spend the rest of the time discussing how it applies to you. Close your meeting by praying to God for wisdom to know how best to apply the things you have learnt.

One other thing. Throughout this book, fictitious little stories are used to illustrate some of the common mistakes in youth work. They are composite stories, and are certainly not meant to be hurtful to our brothers and sisters in ministry. Indeed, most of them are drawn from our own ministries, our own mistakes. We are not the El Supremos of youth ministry. The only reason we know anything is that collectively we have made almost every error described in this book.

Our aim is to encourage you to think carefully and biblically about what you are doing with your youth group. We hope that you will be stimulated to teach the Bible, to encourage evangelism and to make disciples. More than anything, we hope that Jesus will extend his kingdom as a response to our prayers.

Where are all the young people?

Phil grabbed the minister after church. There was something on his mind. The pastor, John Lansdowne, had been at the church for over a year now and Phil had always found him approachable and friendly. Now was the time to share his concern about the youth ministry of the church.

"John, I'm worried because we don't seem to be attracting young people along to our youth groups anymore. I went along on Friday night to see what was happening and I was horrified."

John looked surprised. "This sounds pretty distressing, Phil. I know we don't have the world's biggest youth group, but I didn't know we were in that much trouble."

"Well, that's right—we don't have a very big group, and we should have!" said Phil. "There are plenty of kids in this suburb and we're not attracting them. And on Friday night, I worked out the reason why. All they seemed to do was Bible study. I mean we're talking about high school kids here! They're not going to stick around if we only ever do this heavy stuff."

"It's hard to argue against teaching the Bible in a church youth group," John said, with the merest hint of sarcasm.

"Yeah, but when I was a kid in this church we had a youth group of over 100 people. And we didn't do Bible study. We had games and activities. It was all action, and it was great fun. That's the way to get the kids in. I couldn't believe it when I saw 25 people there on Friday night."

John thought for a moment before he spoke. "Did you really get over 100 people along every Friday night, Phil?"

"Yeah, we did. It was terrific."

"Okay, so tell me—where are they now? Are they still coming?"

Now it was Phil's turn to think for a while.

"They've all moved on. In fact, not many of them still go to church anymore."

"Hmm," said John. "Maybe teaching the Bible to the youth group isn't such a bad idea after all."

What is this book about?

This conversation, or one like it, actually took place. It indicates that there are very different opinions about how youth ministry is to be done. Most churches have a youth group of some kind, but very few have actually worked out what they are doing and why.

Our underlying assumption is that youth ministry is like any other gospel ministry—it is all about the proclamation and teaching of the gospel of Jesus Christ. And this is not an academic exercise. It is about lives which are changed because of Jesus. This book is about how to lead a youth group in which young people grow to maturity in their relationship with Jesus Christ.

Our first four chapters look at the basic goals of youth ministry. If seeing young people brought into the kingdom of God is our starting point, then the next step is to make sure that our group is actually working toward that goal. Having the right goals will affect the programs that we run.

We then look at one of the most important factors in youth ministry (or any ministry)—the model of the leader's life. Chapter five is about good leadership and how it is to be exercised.

Good leaders are also able to develop leadership skills in other people. Jesus chose a small group of people to carry on after he left. While he was still on earth, he worked closely with them so that they would know what to do in the future. In our discipling we should develop other leaders. This will help to build a strong and unified group which is clear in its gospel orientation. This is the subject of chapter six.

Of course, any God-honouring youth group will be concerned with reaching the unsaved outside their group. The strategy for evangelism which we outline in chapter seven aims at training and motivating the members of the group to be evangelistically minded, not just the leaders. We also look at the role of evangelism in the overall youth programme.

Chapters eight and nine discuss some of the nuts and bolts of youth ministry, such as producing an atmosphere of enjoyment and mutual respect. We also look at how to be freed from the tyranny of that perennial youth group activity—games, how to win parental approval for our activities, and how to make best use of camps and weekends away.

The final chapter on sexuality is one of the most important in the book. Satan is always seeking to undermine the work that we are involved in, and one of his best attacks is sexual temptation. Too many effective gospel ministries have been crippled by sexual sin, especially among leaders. We pray that you will consider these words carefully and take them to heart.

But before we go too much further, we need to answer a very basic question: Why should we do youth ministry in the first place?

Good reasons for not doing youth ministry

It may sound strange, but there are lots of good reasons why we should *not* do youth ministry. It doesn't take long to think of other things to do with our time.

For a start, doing youth ministry is not the way to build a big church. Young people don't have much money, and if they do, they won't give it to support the ministry of the church. It just isn't possible to grow a church, in the short-term, by focusing on young people. The economic reality is that young people cannot sustain gospel work by themselves.

Of course, a time will come when they are in a position to leave school and start to gain some financial independence. And what's the song that young people sing as soon as they are independent? *Movin' Out.* Most of the teenagers you work with will grow up and leave the area within the next five years. It's a fact of life—in large cities, it's very hard to buy a house in the same area as your parents. And, of course, if the young people are studying, there is a good chance they will move somewhere close to their university or college.

Even if they don't move away, young people cause problems. Successful youth ministry will change a church. All growth is painful because it inevitably involves change. An influx of young people into a congregation will lead to new ideas, new approaches and new challenges. Try inserting 40 young people into a traditional church service and see what happens. Before too long, there will be tension and pressure to alter the way the service runs. The regular members will be defensive—they were quite happy with the way things were before; they just wanted more people there. Good youth ministry will produce tension because it will produce growth. One way to avoid that tension is not to do good youth ministry.

Everyone knows that young people are often emotionally unpredictable. Youth ministry can be very unrewarding. You can share your life with a group of people, pour your heart out to them, lie awake at night worrying about them—and then find that they let you down and break your heart. Selfishness and instability are the hallmarks of youth.

So why bother?

With a list like that, who would ever bother to get involved in youth ministry? But never fear—there are a few good things about young people too. Indeed, there are even a few good reasons to get involved in gospel work with them.

The first reason for doing youth ministry is the same reason that people keep climbing huge mountains: because they are there. Young people are accessible, available and convertible. And believe it or not, young people (with the possible exception of 14 year olds) are human beings! The gospel is applicable to them too. They too can share in the benefits won by Jesus on the cross. The New Testament never speaks about youth ministry, maybe because people in those days weren't as obsessed with age as we are. The apostles didn't do youth ministry; they just did 'ministry'. So one good reason to evangelize young people is—that they are people!

Perhaps there are even more compelling reasons than this. It's the sort of thing that politicians say around election time, but it's true—young people are the future. Even if your church doesn't grow from youth ministry, the New Testament never tells us to pursue church growth for its own sake. Jesus teaches about the growth of the kingdom of God (Luke 13:18), and Paul talks about the growth of the gospel itself (Col 1).

Our real aim is 'gospel growth', not just the growth of our human structures. And young people are a good investment. A kid converted at 15 can reasonably expect to look forward to at least fifty years on earth to proclaim the gospel. The realization that we are building for the future should be enough by itself to encourage us to invest wisely in the lives of young Christians.

The later teenage years, from about age 15 onwards, can be a very exciting time. It is the time of life when people may well be more open to hearing the message of the gospel than they will be for years to come. They have energy, enthusiasm, idealism and creativity. They are open to new ideas and new challenges. And they keep coming back week after week for more. Since most young people are single, they actually have more opportunity to be involved in the Lord's work than they may ever have again (see 1 Cor 7:32-35). Late adolescence is a rare time in life when people are actually asking the big life question of 'Why?', and they are not yet fettered by jobs, mortgages, and the drudgery of a 9-to-5 existence. Being young often means being open.

If young people are open to the gospel, it also means that they are open to some bad influences too. The media and the world of marketing are after the hearts and souls of kids too, in order to instill a 'Coca-Cola mentality'—that life is all about sun, surf, beautiful people and a relentless devotion to consumerism. The pressure to conform to the love of this world is strong.

The exact nature of this pressure may vary from one geographical area to the next. In some places it will be the pressure to take a very highly paid (and very demanding) job. In another area it might be to leave home and school early and 'veg out'. Those two options may seem worlds apart, but in fact they are the same—the lure of sex, drugs, rock'n'roll, money and pleasure. Christians are not the only people out to win the hearts and minds of young people.

Certainly, God thinks that teaching young people is important. Proverbs 22:6 says: "Train a child in the way he should go and when he is old he will not turn from it". In 2 Timothy, Paul encourages his young friend to persevere in gospel ministry. Indeed Timothy's life had shown the effects of good teaching from a young age: "Continue in what you have learned and become convinced of... from infancy you have known the Holy Scriptures which are able to make you wise for salvation through faith in Christ Jesus" (2 Tim 3:14-15).

When youth ministry is good, it is extremely exciting. There is nothing better than seeing people come to know Jesus as Lord. There is nothing more fulfilling than seeing young people grow to maturity in Christ. When all is said and done, it's great fun to work with them.

But youth ministry isn't easy. Most of us know that only too well from personal experience. It takes time and commitment—but if you weren't committed to the gospel you wouldn't have picked up this book and read this far. Like many things in life, it is true to say of youth ministry: no guts, no glory.

Think about it

1. What things do you like best about doing youth ministry?

2. What things do you like least?

3. What would you say were the best and worst things about your own group? Be constructive: what can you do to fix them?

4. Do people fall away from your church at a certain age? Track some people who have been through your group in the last couple of years and see.

The paradox of youth ministry

What are we aiming for?

The ideal youth group?

The youth ministry at St Jason's had gained quite a reputation during the three years that Sean Lamb had been there. Many young people were contacted and began to attend the Friday night meeting. It was not unusual on those Friday evenings to see the large hall bustling with activity as 50-100 kids joined in. Occasionally, a bus load from another area would arrive to swell the numbers.

Surely this was frontline ministry. Most of these kids were unchurched. Sean's work at St Jason's seemed to be a great success.

So it was with some surprise that Sean listened to what Pastor John Lansdowne had to say.

"Sean, I don't think our youth strategy is working."

"What? We've had our biggest attendance ever over the last couple of months. It's never been better."

"Well, Sean, I know it's getting bigger, but I'm not sure it's getting better. I think you are working hard and doing your best, but we have got some problems. Are you happy with the behaviour on Friday nights?"

"Actually, we do have some problems there, I'll admit that. Some of the kids are pretty rowdy."

"I think they're more than just rowdy; I think they're out of control. I get the impression that we don't change the lives of the non-Christian kids—they change the lives of our Christian kids. The group norm isn't very Christian, and it seems almost impossible to change at this stage. How are your leaders?"

"Yeah, well, they're actually pretty discouraged. They try

hard, but it really is tough trying to get the kids to listen."

"My impression, Sean, is that they are quite burnt out. I've just been speaking to one who says he wants to quit. He feels like our group is more like child-minding than ministry. We never see any of the youth group kids at church, and the Christian parents won't let their kids go because it's so wild. Sean, it's a big group, but are you sure it's a good group?"

Sean was a committed youth worker who really wanted to reach young people with the gospel. But he had made the fatal mistake in youth ministry. He had never actually worked out what he was trying to do and why.

Dump trucks and beads

The approach to youth ministry used by Sean at St Jason's was what we might call the 'dump truck' method. Essentially, this method involves attracting as many outside or non-churched kids as possible to what are basically social events. On any given night, 50, 100, or even 200 kids are dumped on site. The youth leaders then try to evangelize these kids and build a youth group from them.

While it sounds great in theory, we have already seen the in-built problems with this method. The dump truck method is always in a state of tension. The kids come for a good time. As soon as you start trying to teach about Jesus, the good time stops. Therefore, the kids stop coming or stop listening. And why not? The reason they are there is to have fun, isn't it? The result is a group that can, at best, hope to keep some kids off the streets for part of one night a week. Like a lot of social work, it has limited effectiveness. It certainly will not generate committed disciples of Jesus. Christian maturity does not come about by stealth.

The alternative model is to add beads to a necklace. This model aims to start small and build up a group of young people who meet together for the right reasons—that is, to study the Bible and to encourage one another in their Christian lives. And to have fun while they're doing it.

It is necessary to start small in order to establish norms of group behaviour. It is just not possible to enforce these upon a large unwilling group. Of course, the group aims to grow, but *the code of behaviour is never relaxed.*

As a result, growth will necessarily be slower, like adding beads to a necklace. But when new members join, they know what they are joining. It will produce quality growth rather than just numbers. The necklace grows, but the growth doesn't change its shape.

Having outreaches and social occasions is extremely important. There is most certainly a place for them in this model. But they must not be confused with the aim of the group, which is producing Christian disciples.

The centrepiece of our work must be a small group (or groups) where the Bible is taught, where Christ is taken seriously. We can also run other activities where kids have fun, and can invite their friends. In fact, it is good just to have fun together. It is good for kids to see that Christians can have fun together. But there must be some time when the Bible is taken seriously; a time when kids have to stop and think about the claim of Jesus on their lives. Of course, it doesn't mean that all enjoyment must stop when the Bible is opened—far from it. But it does mean that God's Word must lie at the heart of your program.

The paradox of youth ministry

There is a difference between what young people *want* and what young people *need.* The tension between youth *wants* and youth *needs* lies at the heart of youth ministry.

Youth Wants: fun, fun, fun and party, party, party. This means that meeting people of the opposite sex is an important motivator in the teenage years. Kids will even sit through terminally boring church services just to get the opportunity to speak to people of the opposite sex afterwards.

Youth Needs: security and significance. The need for attention and approval is high—teenagers are notoriously insecure.

Consequently, young people crave significant relationships with people who care for them. Young people respond to love. They also respond to a sense of purpose.

Real Youth Needs: to know Jesus Christ as their Lord and Saviour; to become holy, that is, to become like Jesus; to learn and understand the Word of God and how it applies to their lives.

The Paradox of Youth Ministry: the youth group that is built on trying to achieve Youth Wants will achieve neither Wants nor Needs in the long term. However, if youth ministry is built upon meeting Real Youth Needs, the gospel will ultimately provide what young people really need and want.

What are we aiming for?

The place to start in youth ministry is to ask the question: 'What are we actually aiming for?'

As we have already suggested, your aim as a *Christian* youth group leader is to run a group which:

- sees people come into a living relationship with Jesus; and
- sees Christian people move on in their relationship with God to become mature through understanding his character and what he requires of us as revealed in his word.

We could all say 'Amen' to this. It's hard to argue with a set of aims like that.

But despite the very best intentions, it seems that many groups find the theory easier than the practice. Your group might fall into one of these three categories:

1. Someone in the dim dark past set up the current structure, but no-one can remember why. Furthermore, no-one is bold enough to change things, because they've always been done this way.
2. The present program seems to be more geared towards church death than church growth. Everyone wants the

group to grow, but no-one is quite sure how that is going to take place.

3. You belong to a group which attracts masses of teenagers (except when there is a good party on), but little effective work seems to be accomplished for the kingdom of God.

If your group does fall into one of the above categories, then you are a bit like the man who is training the local soccer team. He gathers around himself a group of interested and enthusiastic young people and proceeds to teach them the game. The first problem is that he uses a rugby ball. Then they train on a basketball court. In a short period of time he pulls his hair out when none of his proteges show the least advancement in the game of soccer!

The problem with the soccer trainer is that he failed to set up structures that helped him to achieve his goal of training soccer players. There is a great similarity to many youth groups. While we have noble aims, we never seem to accomplish them because we don't carefully gear our whole program to achieve the goals.

The basic ingredient

The most important ingredient in youth ministry is the word of God. No matter what else happens, we must make sure that the Bible is well taught. When Paul wanted to instruct his young disciple, Timothy, on how to conduct his ministry, he said this:

> In the presence of God and of Christ Jesus, who will judge the living and the dead, and in view of his appearing and his kingdom, I give you this charge: Preach the Word; be prepared in season and out of season; correct, rebuke and encourage—with great patience and careful instruction. (2 Tim 4:1-2)

The Bible must be taught so that young people can understand it. The Bible must be taught so that young people can obey it.

And it must be taught so that they can read it for themselves.

This does not necessarily mean a 30–minute sermon every week, and it certainly does mean that our teaching must never be tedious. There is no excuse for making the exciting news of reconciliation with God as boring as the test pattern on TV. Lecturing is not the only means of teaching. Indeed, with young people, it may be among the least effective. Don't trot out the same routine format every week. Be creative and sensitive to the age and stage of the kids. (For more on teaching the Bible in youth ministry, see the next chapter.)

Our aim is to produce Christian disciples. Therefore, the Bible, God's living word, must be at the centre of everything we do. Every structure or program should be negotiable. But our commitment to Christ and his word must never be negotiable.

So who do I begin with?

All young people are of equal value in terms of gospel work: the drug addict and the prostitute are worth no more and no less than the middle-class kid. Our aim must be to reach the greatest number we can with the gospel. Often that means starting where we are; it also often means working where we will be personally most effective. This may involve starting small and building for the future.

To form a youth group, the one essential thing needed is—a youth. Once you've got one, you're away.

Begin with your own church kids, if for no other reason than that they are already there. They will have been 'Christianised', if not converted, and their parents will be on-side. There is another reason to start with your own church kids—we have an obligation to care for them. It is part of the church's ministry to the whole family. Part of this will mean providing a Christian peer group in which 'churched' teenagers can grow and develop; a place where it is OK to be Christian and to have fun.

Having started with your own church kids, next try to

pick up fringe kids on the edge of your congregation—those who have at least some contact with the church. They may be irregular attenders at church, or confirmation contacts.

From there, try to reach out to the friends of group members. As you pick up new contacts, work your way out. New people open up new networks of friends to invite.

Summary

So far, we have seen that there is only really one reason to do youth ministry—to see young people converted to love and serve the Lord Jesus Christ. And we have seen that the centrepiece of that work is teaching the word of God. But how exactly do you teach the Bible to teenagers?

That is the subject of our next chapter.

What about your group?

1. How would you describe the code of behaviour in your group?

2. When new people join your group, what do you think are their expectations?

3. Take a large piece of paper and draw three concentric circles labelled 'church kids', 'fringe kids' and 'contacts' (moving out from 'church kids' in the centre). Who fits into these circles in your youth ministry?

4. If you removed bible teaching from your program, would anyone notice or care? What about if you removed games?

Prayerfully teaching the Bible

The youth leader's basic task

If you were to compile a list of Christian jargon, then—depending on the sort of church you go to—the phrase 'teaching the Bible' would probably come near the top (just a few points behind 'born again', 'evangelism' and 'bless you, sister'). We admit we've used the phrase several times already in this book.

It has become so common now (in evangelical circles at least) that we're in danger of using it and not knowing what it means, or of misunderstanding it altogether.

It's also a phrase people react to quickly. So, when a speaker encourages his audience of youth leaders to teach the Bible, half of his listeners think: "Yes! That's the best thing we could be doing"; and the other half think: "No! That's the quickest way to bore your youth group to death."

In a similar way, there are plenty of new youth ministry resources that claim to be Bible-based or to help you teach the Bible. Some of them do the job; others among them clearly haven't understood what teaching the Bible is about.

The aim of this chapter is to explain what it is (including tips on how to do it) and why to do it. But it may help first of all to clear up what teaching the Bible is not.

Popular misconceptions
- Teaching the Bible is about giving long talks—generally too long.
- Teaching the Bible involves explaining a Bible passage in great depth (aided by showing you have a knowledge of Greek and Hebrew, an ability to use alliteration and a

refusal to include any relevant illustrations).

- Teaching the Bible means taking little interest in your listeners' needs, interests or concentration span.
- Teaching the Bible means killing off a good Bible story by straining to look for meaning in every word.

According to this way of thinking, Bible teaching is like explaining Shakespeare–an admirable thing to do, and appreciated by a minority, but not what is needed in the 21st century. And indeed, if this is what teaching the Bible really involved, the authors of this book would agree!

Perhaps it's time to see what this business really is all about.

What it really is

Put simply, teaching the Bible means explaining its message: explaining first about the gospel (the momentous news of what God has done in Christ); explaining how to turn to Christ and how to live for him.

This definition makes it possible for most of us, right? Teaching the Bible isn't any more complicated than that, but to do it well takes far more than you might at first think. What's involved? Your words, your prayers, your hard work and your life.

Your words

Firstly, your words. Teaching the Bible to young people will mean taking seriously the need to give them a clear presentation of the gospel. You will want to make clear about God being creator of the world, us humans choosing to reject that loving rule over us, and God in his holiness rightly condemning us to be separated from him forever. You'll want to explain Jesus' coming to die in our place, his being separated from God for us, his being raised to life as Lord of all, and the offer of eternal life, forgiveness and a relationship with God.

In other words, teaching the Bible involves explaining its message–as it's given in the Bible. So we present the gospel as the Bible presents it: Christ died for our sins (1 Cor 15:3). So it's worth checking that we've included all the elements of the gospel that the Bible does, and that we're emphasising the aspects that we should be.

For example, we're often tempted to tell young people how severe the physical suffering of Jesus was on the cross. But the Bible doesn't do that: instead, it concentrates on how awful it was for Jesus, God's Son, to be separated from his Father, under his condemnation. And it says that he went through that for us.

Explaining this carefully, attractively, clearly and at a level your young people can grasp will also mean you'll need to check yourself. Have you understood this gospel clearly? Have you taken it in? Can you explain the tremendous achievement of Jesus' death?

It will also mean you don't want to hurry it. Bashing through these major truths in one youth group session once every four years is clearly way off the mark. If the gospel is the way that people will be rescued for God for eternity, then explaining it often is essential, isn't it?

What a disaster it would be if some young person came to your youth group for three weeks only and went away without hearing any mention of Jesus and the cross. The onus will be on you, the youth leader, to keep your explanations of the gospel continually fresh and relevant.

Your prayers

Teaching the Bible is not simply an intellectual activity, although it does take hard intellectual work (as we will see below). It is a spiritual activity. God's word is a mighty weapon, but it is only effective when it is wielded by God himself through his Spirit (see Eph 6:17-18). Those who teach are like gardeners who plant and water; it is God who provides the growth (1 Cor 3:6-7). We may prepare and lead the finest Bible study in the history of Christian youth ministry, but if God is not working in the hearts of those who hear it, our fine words and telling illustrations will bounce off like golf balls off a concrete bunker.

It is to God, then, that we must turn in prayer as a vital part of all Bible teaching. Like Paul, we should pray that we would teach boldly and clearly, as we should (Eph 6:19-20; Col 4:2-3). But we should pray mainly for those who hear the message: that God would enable them to receive the word, and embrace it and bear fruit; that God would lift the veil from their eyes, and shine his light in their hearts (2 Cor 4:1-6). Bible teaching is a supernatural work; it must be surrounded by prayer.

This means praying for the kids in your group regularly, and by name. Don't spend four hours preparing your study, and then mutter a quick 'Help me, Lord' as you arrive. Put aside some time, as part of your preparation, to pray not only for yourself (in rightly understanding and teaching the passage), but for the kids, that God would work in their lives. Pray for their particular spiritual struggles. Pray that the particular message you are preparing would change them, and that they would persevere in the truth.

Prayer is not easy–Paul describes it as being a wrestling match (Col 4:12)–but it is vital. And that brings us to the subject of hard work.

Your hard work

Explaining the Bible's message as it's given in the Bible will drive us to work hard at each Bible passage. After all, each of its 66 books was written at a particular time for particular people in a particular way. Good questions to ask would be: What's the main thrust of this book? How does this passage fit into it? Why does it say that here? What's happened before and after? How does it all fit together? What did it mean for its first readers? How does it help me understand Jesus better? What are the implications for us now?

So we work hard at finding out what a verse or paragraph or chapter of the Bible is actually saying, understanding what it means in its context and then working out how to explain and apply it relevantly to ourselves and our hearers.

The Bible gives us great encouragement as we do this hard work: that as we come humbly and prayerfully to grapple with the Bible, so God promises to give us insight into it by his Spirit. What a privilege! Teaching the Bible really is the best job in the world.

Sadly, too many youth group speakers have got lazy. They find a verse they like and then rabbit away without really explaining it (or, horribly, they find what they think is a great illustration and work it into their teaching even if it's got nothing to do with the Bible verse they've chosen).

This usually results in most talks ending up with an appeal for the young people to be more committed, to pray more, to read their Bibles more and to be better witnesses to their friends.

All of those things are worth encouraging in your young people (well, those who are Christians), but misusing the Bible like this is a surefire way merely to get repetitive, or worse, just to preach your latest hobby-horses. And most seriously, it will mean that you and your youth group miss out on all that God has for us in the Bible: the great truths, warnings, encouragements, examples and promises that are expressed through the Bible's varied human writers.

Those who adopt this teaching approach of working hard at each Bible passage will quickly find the joy and usefulness of working through a Bible book consecutively. What better way to build up your Christian young people than by teaching them—carefully and attractively—the letters of 1 Thessalonians, Colossians or Philippians, for example? What better way to help them get to know Jesus than to dive into one of the four gospels at a pace and level they can handle?

We've listed at the end of this chapter a number of methods to help you teach the Bible well to young people. Choose, use and adapt. The important thing is 'stay on message' (as politicians put it), but to keep adapting the form to suit your young people. It is an unfortunately common mistake for 20-year-old youth leaders to lead Bible discussions that are great for 20-year-olds, but too long and too high-powered for the eight 13-year-olds in their small group.

So, teaching the Bible means explaining its message as it is given in the Bible. But this job isn't limited merely to those times when we're 'up-front'. Teaching the Bible means making use of all the teaching opportunities that we have with our young people: your small group work, your one-to-one discipling, your casual social contact, and so on. In fact, every conversation you have can be a teaching opportunity: not a lecturing opportunity, but a moment to point people naturally to Jesus.

There's no excuse for overdoing it, or boring people, but we suspect most Christians go too far the other way and rarely say anything about Jesus in daily conversation. That's something to be remedied: pray for opportunities to teach about Jesus and take them.

Your life

But if we're to teach well, we'll use more than just words. Explaining the Bible's message involves our lives. It involves letting young people in on our lives. It's not just a 'words to ears' ministry, but a 'life to life' one.

Young people will learn most from us not by hearing every talk we've ever done, but by seeing us live out what we're teaching. So, when you're teaching about Jesus as Lord, that message will come home strongly when a member of your youth group sees you at home, making everyday choices about how to spend time and money and energy.

Equally, teaching about marriage (we hope you teach this to your young people) will be greatly reinforced (or undermined) by the way you relate to your wife/husband, children and wider family.

The precedent for this is Jesus, and we see it too in the way the apostles went about their teaching ministry. Jesus chose twelve disciples essentially 'to be with him' over a concentrated three year period. They would have seen him practically 24 hours a day: eating, sleeping, travelling, teaching, praying, chatting, the lot.

Out of those twelve, Jesus seemed to choose three (Peter, James and John) for a particularly close friendship. Possibly out of them it was Peter who received more personal attention and training. And it's clear that Jesus seemed to go out of his way to let those disciples see him at his moments of need (such as in the Garden of Gethsemane).

Paul adopted this pattern too: he could tell the Thessalonian church that he had shared with them not just the gospel of God, but his life as well (1 Thes 2:8).

Do you see the implications for youth leadership? Open your life up, including your home. Perhaps concentrate your energies on just two or three individuals (the same sex as you) whom you will seek to bring to Christ, nurture and train. Let them see you trusting Christ and living for him in everyday life, and resist the urge to keep pretending you're always calm and competent: let them see you when you're struggling with decision-making, finding prayer hard, juggling that overloaded diary, and too tired to answer the phone.

This is what teaching the Bible rightly will always involve. Explaining its message will mean living it out, for you can't explain it unless you have truly understood it; and you can't truly understand it if you're not living it out. Be diligent to walk closely with Christ and let your young people in on that. If all you're doing as a youth leader is rolling up for a meeting once a week, then you're not teaching the Bible anywhere near as effectively as you could be. The way you spend time outside the meeting is as important as what you do in the meeting itself.

All this may mean that the youth worker or older youth leaders run 'open house'—and kids can drop in anytime. This may work well and will probably be popular, but it may actually hinder effective, concentrated work with a few—and you might find it hard to achieve anything else at home early on. Why not set aside a certain number of afternoons or evenings in the week when people can drop around?

Or, perhaps better still, let that handful of people become more a part of your life: it doesn't take more meetings, evenings or organizing. Simply let them join in what you're up to: you need to eat—so mealtimes are an obvious easy opportunity. Do you have to go to the supermarket, cut the hedge, wash the car, or buy a birthday present? Take one of your young people, too: involve them in your life without watching the clock. You'll find it surprising how ready they are to join in what seem to be the most mundane adult activities. Over time—and it may take years to build this up—your influence on them, teaching them the Bible, can be profound.

Certainly, there is need to act wisely here and to be above reproach. Early on, choose carefully who comes round and make sure their parents know what you will be doing. Watch your behaviour with these young people: intimate one-to-one counselling behind a closed upstairs door at home is not on; inviting a small group round can be a safeguard for them as much as for you. Be 'public' even at home: let there be no situation which could be mis-read. If the door-bell goes or the phone rings and you're embarrassed about what's going on, then sort things out fast.

Doing your youth work like this—sharing your life—will mean that these young people become your friends. It will mean, most likely, taking on a friend for life. What an opportunity!

If you want to save your young people, and feed them and see them grow as Christians, then prayerfully teach them the Bible: it's that alone that will encourage, correct, rebuke, train and change their lives like nothing else. It's the Bible that is God's word to us. So do more than just dip into it as a reference book. Teach it: with your words, your prayers, your hard work and your life.

Bible-teaching should be the central activity of your youth

ministry, but it will not be the only one. How does Bible teaching fit into the wider program of what we do? In our next two chapters, we move on to look at how to set basic goals for your youth ministry, and construct a program to achieve them.

Think about it

1. Think of the person or people that taught you the gospel. Are there any lessons to draw from the way they did it?

2. In youth work, what are the alternatives to teaching the Bible? What makes these attractive? What are their pitfalls? What priority should they have?

3. What things get in the way of praying for your youth group?

4. As a result of reading this chapter, what changes need to be made by a) you; b) the youth work you're involved in? Where are you going to start?

Creative ideas for teaching the Bible to young people

● Agree/disagree: The leader voices one or more statements on a subject; students indicate whether they agree or disagree with the statements. Stimulates thinking.

● Brainstorming: This involves listing as many ideas as possible on a given subject or problem, without evaluation.

● Buzz groups: The leader divides the group into several small groups for discussion or special study.

● Case study: A description of a real life problem situation is presented; the group analyzes the problem and suggests a solution. Builds problem-solving skills and helps members gain insights into life.

● Circle response: Each member, beginning with one person and continuing around the group, 'airs' his opinion or answer to a question. Allows each person to express an opinion.

● Debate: Negative and positive sides present opposing views on an issue. Arguments and rebuttals are given alternately. Stimulates thought and discussion.

● Demonstration: One or several members demonstrate how to perform a specific task or skill; afterwards, others are given the opportunity to practice what they've observed.

● Direct Bible Study: This method is essential, especially when studying a key Scripture passage. It involves getting group members into a study of the Word itself. They get practice in how to study the Bible as you guide them in finding out what a passage really says, what it means, and how it applies to them.

* Discussion: The leader asks stimulating questions, and the group members exchange their opinions. The leader should guide the group to some definite conclusions.
* Field trip: The group visits a museum, mission, church, home or other location to gain knowledge or insight. Later, group members discuss what they observed.
* Illustrations: Interesting incidents, brief stories, and real or imaginary applications, often illuminate truth for teenagers.
* Interview: The leader (or a capable group member) interviews another person, asking him questions, or learning his opinions on certain issues. This may be done outside group time and recorded on a cassette to play to the group.
* Key questions: When studying a Scripture passage, reviewing important facts, or discussing practical problems, it is important to bring out *key ideas* by asking good questions (ones that are thought-provoking and can't be answered with 'yes' or 'no'). Leaders should word their questions carefully and write them out in their notes.
* Lecture summary: Often it is helpful to present certain facts, or to summarize part, or all, of the lesson by means of lecture. Whenever a leader does the talking, he should be enthusiastic and speak on a level that young people understand. Most leaders need to be careful that they don't lecture too much.
* Listening teams: Assign groups to watch for various emphases or answers to questions as given by a speaker, film, etc.
* Neighbour nudging: A group is divided into pairs to discuss a particular question—usually for one minute only.
* Panel: Three to five people discuss a subject informally. In a symposium, each member speaks on a restricted part of

the topic. In a forum, experts answer questions from the audience.

* Project: An individual or group plans and carries out a specific task or service, usually as the result of an application of Bible principles.

* Research reports: During the week, the leader assigns a capable group member to present a report on a given topic, perhaps on background material or one phase of the lesson. The leader should provide some help in finding reference books, etc.

* Role play: A problem is acted out, with individuals identifying as much as possible with the characters; a discussion of the situation follows.

* Scripture search: This is a good way to find out what the Bible says about a topic or doctrine. It is usually best to write out the various references on slips of paper. The leader passes out the verses and calls on each member to read and/or explain a verse.

* Skit: A dramatic presentation of an event or situation to set a tone or illustrate a point.

* Team teaching: Several people, or perhaps a couple, may co-operate and lead a study. The teaching responsibilities may be divided and shared in a variety of ways.

* Testing: A leader motivates and checks up on how his group is learning by using quizzes (written or oral, formal or informal).

* Visuals: A leader can multiply his effectiveness by appealing to the 'eye-gate' through charts, maps, pictures or physical objects. The blackboard is also an important means of visualizing. Young people can also learn by seeing interesting bulletin boards, books, magazines, and missionary curios in their room.

How to avoid punching the air

Setting goals and achieving them

Friday night, a youth group somewhere...

The younger members of the youth group were the first to arrive back to the hall. They burst in with great exuberance and the sure knowledge that they had won the chalk chase. Over the next 15 minutes, the rest of the youth group piled back in. They were shouting, laughing and jostling one another as they recounted tales of car alarms set off, shopping trolleys borrowed (with the possibility of three kids inside and a gently sloping street—who could resist the temptation?), and every unsuspecting granny in the area trampled under six pairs of feet. The game was a huge success—LET'S DO IT AGAIN NEXT WEEK!

The leaders settled the kids down for the next two events on the program—singing and the Bible study. The hesitant guitarist/song-leader stood up to lead the group in *God said to Noah there's gonna be a floody-floody*. After what seemed like an eternity of poor singing, rowdiness and general disinterest in whatever God said to whom, the disillusioned song-leader sat down.

The leader rose to give his Bible study. It was a study on the parables. Tonight's topic was "Being ready for the return of Jesus". It was well-prepared, relevant and delivered in a manner which was certainly not a disaster. Those who listened gained a lot out of it, and there were some who even took notes. Upon reflecting on his talk, however, the leader felt discouraged. "They didn't seem to listen", he told himself. "In fact they often don't listen. Oh well, maybe next Friday things will be different."

This fictional tale may have a ring of truth about it. It's a generalisation, but still true, that many youth groups are small, not growing and beset by problems: a lack of discipline, a failure to reach the unchurched, and the very important problem of kids who drop out of the group when they leave high school.

Is there any solution?

This chapter sets out to provide a simple framework to help you think through the overall direction of your youth group. Where are you headed? Do you have a plan? Or do you feel like you're going round in circles?

There's an old saying: if you aim at nothing, you're sure to hit your target. To avoid that 'punching the air' feeling, try the following three steps.

Step 1: Ask the right questions

Before you do anything else, have a good, close look at each and every part of your program and ask the following sorts of questions.[1]

Why are we doing this? What do we hope to achieve by it? In the end, will it be destructive or constructive for God's kingdom? Are we doing this simply because it has always been done this way? Or are we doing it just because somebody in the group suggested it and one or two others said, "Yeah, that sounds great"?

These are hard questions, but they are the first step towards working out what you should be doing and why. You will be amazed at how far this simple process can take you. Just stopping to ask the questions often makes the answers obvious.

Take Bill, for example. He has just taken over the leadership of a medium-sized, vibrant youth group. On Sunday nights after church, virtually the whole group goes back to someone's house for supper (usually an on-the-spot volun-

---

1. *Mission Minded*, by Peter Bolt, is an excellent resource to help you in this process (and in steps 2 and 3 following). It is available from Matthias Media.

teer). Within five minutes of the service finishing, the word has got around and within another five minutes the church is just about empty.

Bill sits down one night and does some thinking. He realizes that there is no real reason for these after-church suppers. They just 'happened' a couple of times, and before long they were a regular event. The suppers do build feelings of warmth and closeness among the core of the youth group, and Bill is pleased about that.

However, he is also a bit concerned. One of his main goals is for the youth group to grow through evangelism, and in particular through the members inviting their friends to church. But Bill has noticed that when newcomers do come, they never seem to make it to the suppers. Perhaps they find the idea of going to a stranger's house a little threatening—in any case, the same people always seem to go to the suppers, and the newcomers are left behind in an empty church (but not for long—they quickly leave).

After thinking about what he would really like to achieve at church, Bill decides to try something different. He starts to run suppers in the church building straight after church. The supper is laid out attractively, so that as people mingle they tend to gravitate towards the supper tables.

The result is that everybody hangs around a lot longer, including the newcomers. Encouraged by the non-threatening environment, the newcomers start to engage in a bit more conversation with the Christians. Bill then trains several people to be his 'welcomers'. Their job is to spot any newcomers or 'fringe-dwellers', welcome them, get them a cup of coffee, introduce them to a few people, and so on. These 'welcomers' might have to forsake chatting with their own friends until later on in the evening.

Bill received a few complaints about the demise of the home suppers. But he knew what he wanted to achieve and he explained this to the disgruntled members in the hope that they would catch the vision and support him. Eventually, most of them did.

It isn't easy to do what Bill did. But then again, who said that youth ministry (or any ministry) was easy? It takes some thought, some time, and often some guts. But if you don't start by asking the right questions, you won't find the right answers.

Try asking some hard questions about *your* youth group. Choose any three of your current activities and use the following table to 'ask the right questions'.

	Activity 1	Activity 2	Activity 3
Why are we doing it?			
Why was it set up in the first place?			
What is it accomplishing?			

Step 2: Set some goals

This may sound like a fairly obvious step, but judging by the number of youth groups that overlook it, it needs to be said! Beyond the general aim of seeing people converted and built up, many leaders have no specific goals at all.

To be an effective leader, you must take time to *think about where you want to go*. In Step 1 (above), you have looked at your current activities and asked yourself 'why'. The next step is to formulate what you would like to achieve–i.e. your goals. There are different sorts of goals:

Numbers

Have you thought about how many people you would like to have in your group in twelve months time? If the group is very inward looking, you might want to see a significant increase in numbers. You might want the group to start inviting their friends more and telling them about Jesus.

On the other hand, you might want to see a *decrease* in numbers if you have a large, unruly group with a high percentage of people who have no interest in Jesus and are simply there to socialise.

It is not always right to have numerical growth as your goal, but you need to think about it.

The End Product

Have you thought about what sort of people you want the members of your youth group to be in one, two, or five years time? What sort of impact do you want to have on their lives? For example, you might make it a goal that within 18 months you will have 75% of the group established as stable Christians, with a good understanding of the basic truths of the gospel.

Providing leadership

If your youth group is to ever grow beyond 35, you will need other leaders to work alongside you. And a day will come when these up-and-coming leaders will have to take on your mantle of leadership. Where are these leaders going to come from? And how will they be trained? It is always worth setting goals in this area.

In a general sense, we all have the same goal: to glorify God and extend his kingdom. But when it comes down to specific goals, it is not for us to tell you what to do. There is a wide variety of perfectly legitimate, godly goals you can set, and what you come up with will depend on your own particular circumstances. It is up to you to think about your situation and map out some appropriate goals for, say, the next twelve months.

Just to give you some ideas, here is a sample set of goals worked out by our old friend Sean Lamb at St Jason's. Again, we'd like to stress that these may not be right for *your* situation—they are just an example.

Goals for the St Jason's Youth Group for this year

Our group has large numbers of 'fringe-dwellers' who come along on Friday night, but aren't very committed. Quite a few of those who are Christians are fairly unstable and don't have a very good grasp of what it means to be a Christian. Therefore, our goals for this year will be as follows:

- *We will aim to expand the Christian core* of the group from 25 to 35 people—an overall increase of 10.
- We will aim to make sure that these 35 people all know the basic truths of the gospel and are seeking to live them out.
- Since many of our existing core of 25 are children of the congregation at St Jason's, we will aim to provide a satisfying Christian peer group for these kids.
- We will also aim to train four new people to join the leadership team next year (to replace the two that we know will be leaving).

A final word about goals—like many things, they are great servants but lousy masters. Setting goals (like the ones above) is extremely valuable in giving a sense of purpose and direction to your whole youth ministry. With a well thought out set of goals, you have a basis for making progress.

However, if you don't meet your goals, don't lose too much sleep over it. Goal-setting is a great tool, but in the end we must remember that it is God who provides the growth (see 1 Cor 3:5-9). Our job is to ask the right questions, set some appropriate goals, work hard to achieve them, and pray hard that God will bless our efforts. But that's where our responsibility ends. We can't change peoples' lives—only God has the power to do that.

Step 3: Work out a plan to achieve your goals

So far, you've asked the right questions and then set yourself some goals. The next step is obvious: you need to work out a plan to meet your goals. Goals are not like microwave ovens—you can't just 'set and forget'. You must have a workable plan of attack.

You can work out your plan of attack in two ways:

* from your existing program; or
* from a blank piece of paper.

If you start with your *existing program*, then you need to think through each activity to see if it helps or hinders you in achieving your goals. This is really just carrying on from what you did in Step 1 (Asking the right questions). In Step 1, you looked at some of your activities and asked: Why are we doing this? What is it accomplishing?

Now you need to look at each activity and ask: Well, given that we now have these goals, how does this activity fit in? How can it be changed or improved so that it helps to meet our goals? Should it be scrapped (since it doesn't contribute anything to our goals)?

Some areas of your program to examine might be:

* the timing and location of your main meeting
* the length and content of the meeting
* the place of social outings
* small group work
* training leaders
* the frequency of planning meetings
* group behaviour and expectations/discipline
* evangelism

The *blank piece of paper* approach is just as useful, and is worth doing once in a while. It involves getting the youth leadership team together to construct a plan from scratch. That's where the blank piece of paper comes in. You look at your goals and ask: If we were starting from scratch, with none of our existing programs or activities, how would we go about reaching these goals?

The great value of the 'blank piece of paper' method is that it promotes new ideas. Rather than simply tinkering with the existing program, you wipe the slate clean and start again. This process is very good for highlighting those aspects of the program that have been around for ages but no longer contribute towards your goals. You can utter heretical things like: "Well, what if we ran our main meeting on Monday nights?" or "Maybe the best way to achieve goal X would be to start an after-school club on Wednesday afternoons".

Whichever method you use, the important thing is to work out a plan that is designed to meet your goals.

By way of example, here is the plan that Sean Lamb and his leadership team worked out for St Jason's.

Plan for St Jason's Youth Group for this year

- Since we already have a large number of 'fringe' contacts, we won't try to contact any new people this year. Instead, we will concentrate on trying to see our existing contacts become committed Christian members. (We expect to lose about five Christian members during the year, so we will need to gain 15 committed members to reach our target of 35.)
- We will use our Friday night meeting mainly to provide a social outlet for the Christian kids of the congregation. We won't try to do much teaching/discipling on Friday nights, but we will have regular presentations of the gospel so that the 'fringe' members who aren't Christians can be converted.

- We will try to direct as many as possible to the Sunday afternoon meeting before church, where we'll concentrate on Bible study and prayer. We will work particularly hard at recruiting people for this Sunday afternoon group during the first 3–4 months of the year, and then start a series of 'Basic Bible Studies' that outline the gospel and the basic elements of the Christian life.
- We will follow this up in August with a camp that will have as its theme: If you were put on trial for being a Christian, would you be found guilty?
- Four people will be chosen as potential leaders. Members of the current leadership team will meet individually with these four trainees once a fortnight to build them up and train them. Later in the year (around November) we will have a weekend away just for the current leaders and the four trainee leaders, to train and encourage them and set the vision for next year.

Having worked out a plan (like the one above), you will need to review your progress at different times during the year—perhaps at the end of each school term. You will need to stop and ask each other: "OK, we started out at the beginning of the year trying to do X. How are we going?"

In our next chapter, we will continue to look at how to construct your program once you have set your goals. But first, take out some blank paper and write a set of goals and a rough working plan for your own youth group.

The when and how of youth ministry

Successful programming

Imagine for a moment that you are writing your doctoral thesis on 'the nature and substance of Christian youth groups'. You put together a team of researchers to record systematically what takes place in the program of every youth group large and small in every nook and cranny in the land!

After a mammoth effort, you complete your research and arrive at an interesting conclusion. While there might be great differences in terms of activities, timing, venues and so on, there seems to be a marked uniformity in what takes place under the banner of Christian youth ministry. This doesn't really surprise you, because you know that there are certain things that Christians usually do when they meet together. In one way or another, most Christian groups sing, pray, study the Bible and share about their Christian lives. Very few groups meet together to learn juggling, practice taxidermy, or discover the fun of origami.

Basic programming

It appears that there are certain key ingredients which usually make up the Christian youth 'program'. These ingredients vary in form, but in their most basic form they are:

- Singing
- Praying
- Games
- Bible Studies
- Small group work
- Social outings
- Evangelistic gatherings

The crucial question that needs to be asked is *when* and *how* these basic ingredients are placed together. This process of arranging your basic ingredients is 'programming'.

In our last chapter, we looked at the importance of setting clear, gospel-centred goals for your group and taking positive steps to achieve them. Programming is one part of this. Like everything else you do in your group, the way you structure your program must be determined by your *goals*. Good programming happens on two levels.

First, there is the 'macro' program. This is the big picture, the flow of events from February to December. Over the course of a year, the leaders should try to link the various events together to help them reach their goals for the year. They should map out a program incorporating all the components—things like camps, socials, weekly Bible studies, evangelistic meetings, leadership training, and so on.

The other level of programming is the 'micro' level. Here the leaders scrutinize the main meeting of the week (whether it is Friday night or Sunday afternoon or whenever) and try to maximize its effectiveness. The important things here include the flow of the meeting, the expectations of the group, how long it all takes, and how much time is allocated to each component. Do not be tempted to underestimate the importance of this—it is the nuts and bolts of your 'macro' program.

What makes a successful program?

Every youth group in every church in every part of the world has a 'program' (or structure). Some seem to work well—others are less successful.

There is no single 'right' program, nor is there one easy formula for success. There are many variables that will dictate the structure of programming, both at the micro and macro levels. As a leader, it is your job to identify and use these variables to structure the best program for your group.

The following three models may give you something to work from. Each of these models is presently in use with varying degrees of success. It is up to you—the leader—to identify how the strengths and weaknesses of these models apply to your own situation.

Model A

This common pattern is based around a Friday night fellowship meeting. This meeting usually runs from 7.30 pm until around 9.30 pm and includes singing, games, a talk and small groups. There is usually coffee afterwards either at the church hall or at someone's house. The goals of this meeting are to attract young people and to provide a place where they are exposed to Christianity. Many groups using this model also run Sunday discipleship groups before church to accommodate the keener Christians who may not be getting 'fed' by the Friday meetings. On a yearly basis, the program also includes an annual camp, various socials and periodical youth services on Sunday night. (These activities are assumed to take place in Models B and C as well and will not be repeated).

Positives:

- Young people are usually looking for things to do on a Friday night, and therefore attracting new members may not be difficult.
- When working properly, this model has a good 'funnelling' effect. It can bring people to faith through the Friday meeting and into discipleship through the Sunday meeting.
- A Friday night meeting gives the leader a good long stretch of time to work with. Two hours is enough time to do most things and there is rarely a problem of 'fitting everything in'.

Negatives:

- While Friday night may attract young people who have nothing to do, in our culture, many people see Friday night as 'party night' and the time to 'rage'. This attitude may be carried over into the youth group. Thus, it may often be difficult to get anything serious achieved.
- For much the same reason, you may find your meeting time competing with high school musicals, debating competitions, and so on. If a party happens to coincide with your meeting, you might find your numbers down considerably!
- By Friday night, leaders are often tired after a week of study or work. This may hamper their ability to minister effectively.
- Since there is a large amount of time to be filled (sometimes up to two hours), the meeting can be 'unfocused'. To keep young, distracted minds on the job, the meeting rolls quickly from games to singing to prayer time to talk to supper. The whole thing may begin to resemble more of a 'Christian activities night' than a chance for non-Christians to hear the good news.

Model B

This type of program has a Friday night meeting similar to Model A, but it alternates fortnightly. On one week, there is the typical 'Friday night fellowship' to attract, evangelize, and build up the Christians (to a certain extent). On the next week, the model changes and there are 'home groups'. These are small Bible study groups with an emphasis on sharing, prayer, and discipleship through teaching the Word. These Bible studies are run by the various leaders and held in either their home or the homes of the members themselves.

Positives:

- The fortnightly home groups offer a solid time of discipleship training and deeper Bible study. Run properly, these groups offer a chance for the 'full-on' Christians to share and grow together. They also provide an opportunity for 'seekers' to come and enquire more fully about the faith.
- The home groups also provide a warm atmosphere where people can feel part of a group. This must not be underestimated—many young people feel somewhat lost, and need some sort of group to feel part of. They crave a non-threatening environment in which they share with others and hear about God. It is interesting to note that in many places where this type of program is in operation, the numbers are actually *greater* on the night of the home groups.
- Another positive element is that the home groups provide an opportunity to 'get into the homes' of the youth group members. Especially if the member comes from a non-Christian family, this is a great chance to meet the parent(s) and allow them to see exactly what sort of people their son or daughter is mixing with.

Negatives:

- You have many of the same drawbacks as Model A. Since there is still the fortnightly, large-scale meeting, there are the same negatives to contend with.
- There is still the problem of having your main meeting on a Friday night. In some areas (and this is dictated by geography and culture), this may not be a problem, but in other areas it can be a killer.
- To make this model work, the youth group needs to have a number of willing and able leaders. Since this program hinges on its home groups, each home group must have a devoted leader who is committed to discipling his or her charges. The Model B youth group is only as strong as its leaders.

Model C

This model is different in that the main meeting is moved away from Friday night and held on Sunday afternoon before church. The home groups are also different in that they are held weekly instead of fortnightly, usually during the week.

The Sunday meeting has a dual purpose. Since it is before church, many of the young people will stay back and 'follow on'. Therefore, the meeting is designed both to edify the Christian and to help the non-believer discover what it means to be a Christian. As there isn't much time to fill, the meeting tends to be punchy and fast-paced. The program is comprised of the standard ingredients—singing, prayer, Bible study and small groups. The focus, however, is on more general Christian themes. The specific, in-depth Bible studies are left for the small groups that meet mid-week.

These mid-week Bible studies are where the 'real' discipleship takes place. It is an opportunity for the young people to learn and share together under the leadership of an older, mature Christian.

This leaves Friday nights free: social events purely for fun can be scheduled as often as the leaders choose. This helps develop a 'Christian peer group' for kids as they grow up.

Positives:
- Having the main meeting followed by church gives the young people a large amount of Christian input in a relatively short space of time. When this is followed up with a mid-week Bible study, it means that the committed member of the group is gaining plenty of strong, Christian encouragement week by week.
- Since the main meeting is held before church, there is no longer the problem of filling in time (as there might be on a Friday night). If planned and executed properly, the meeting can be fast-paced and enjoyable. It is easy to retain a clear focus.
- Rightly or wrongly, Sunday is seen by many to be 'church day'. Since many (if not most) of the youth group will be planning to go to church anyway, the added youth group meeting before church will probably fit well into their schedule.

Negatives:
- Some young people (and their parents) may find that going to church for four or five hours on a Sunday night is too much. While the combined total is no greater than a Friday night program plus Sunday night church (in fact it is less), some could see it as 'too much in one hit'.
- There could be a problem with the mid-week Bible studies. In some areas, the kids are eager to get out during the week, but in other

situations—especially where there is intense study pressure—
anything organized mid-week could meet with opposition.
- Trying to mix edification and evangelism in the one Sunday meeting
  may also be difficult. Some would argue that it is possible to run only
  one type of meeting effectively—either a meeting designed to edify
  the saints, or one designed to evangelize the unbeliever. To try to mix
  the two is difficult but not impossible.

Three golden rules for successful programming
1. The correct program is the one that helps you achieve your goals

Each aspect of your youth program must be reviewed to see if it is contributing towards your goals.

Take, for example, the goal of conversion growth. You, as the leader, decide that one of your goals is to see ten unchurched young people come to the group (through their Christian friends) and then become Christians. Obviously, this is a great goal. However, if after eight months you realize that there have been no new friends coming into the group, then some rethinking is called for. It may be something quite simple, such as the meeting being held at a bad time. Or it may be a bit more complex—perhaps the current group is too tight and seen by outsiders as a 'clique'.

While not all youth group problems can be solved by programming changes, many can. One youth leader set up a youth group designed to build up the 12–15 years old kids in the church. The goal of the program was to minister mainly to the children of the adults who were attending the morning service. It was hoped that the kids would bring their friends and that through this the group would grow.

The meeting was set up for Friday nights from 7.00 pm to 9.00 pm. What happened was beyond the wildest expectations of the leaders. There was massive, immediate growth. The 'youth club' soon had the reputation of a 'rage' and it was seen by many of the local youth as something to do on an otherwise boring Friday night. The meetings became pandemonium. The weekly Bible message was greeted with boos and a volley of paper and pencils!

The leaders didn't have the facilities to accommodate this sudden growth, so they did a quick rethink and took action. They changed the meeting to Sunday mornings, to be at the same time as the morning service.

In the end, this simple change made all the difference. It immediately removed the unwanted aura of 'a rage'. (Who wants to rage on Sunday mornings at 9.15!) The kids who came along were either forced to by their church-going parents, or were genuinely interested Christian kids, or were friends of the above. While the change brought with it a few minor problems to iron out (such as making sure the leaders got enough sleep each Saturday night!), it helped the group achieve the goals set at the beginning of the year.

This is crucial—if your program is not meeting your goals, change your program (or re-assess your goals).

2. Ineffective programming can destroy the noblest of goals

This is the reverse of Golden Rule #1. Many youth programs carry a lot of 'baggage' in their week-to-week, month-to-month programming. Very often, the program needs to be 'tightened up' because it is hindering the achievement of the group's goals.

Take, for instance, the hallowed 'social'. Many groups decide that it would be fun to get together on a regular basis just to have fun. Regular nights are set aside (e.g. the third Friday of the month) to go bowling, hear a Christian rock band, and so on. On the surface, this sounds great.

The danger lies in the *goals* you set for these nights out. If the goal is to provide a night of fun for the members of the fellowship group on a regular basis, then well and good. If, however, your goal is to increase numbers through inviting friends, there can be trouble. Socials are not always a good vehicle for growth.

Most high-school-aged young people are looking for something to do on weekends and the chance to go out with a group of people their own age (i.e. meeting the opposite sex!) is often too tough to pass up. If a young man or woman comes to a social and then follows on by coming to the weekly meeting, he or she may well be coming to the weekly meeting for the very same reasons they came to the social. Their expectations will not be met, and they will tend to distract the group from its real purpose. Remember, Christian youth groups are there to proclaim Christ to the unbeliever, and disciple the believer. They are not places to meet the opposite sex and fill up your social calendar. Many a youth group has been destroyed by a surge of new people who have come to the group with the wrong motives.

There may be a simple solution to this problem. The leader knows that the group members have a strong need for social interaction. He also knows that there are some dangers in having a 'happening social calendar'. Therefore, he encourages the members to bring their friends to the meeting where the gospel is proclaimed. He regularly schedules meetings designed purely as 'bring a friend nights' where an evangelistic speaker shares the gospel. The socials are still organized, but are limited to group *members* only, or to a very limited number of non-Christian guests. These socials become what they set out to be—nights for the Christians to go out with each other and have a good time.

Three further things need to be said. Firstly, you can't stop people coming to a youth group for the wrong reasons. People are very good at learning Christian jargon and praying with sincere faces just so they can be accepted and enjoy the fringe benefits of the group (e.g. lots of friends, a healthy social life, etc.). You can, however, try to limit this as much as possible.

Secondly, you must be prepared to take criticism if you limit the socials to youth group members only. It will be seen as elitist and snobbish. You must be willing to put up with criticism—it is a small price to pay compared to the danger of having loads of people attending the group for the wrong reasons.

Lastly, bear in mind that social activities perform the important function of building a group of Christian friends, and making it easier for kids to 'own' Christianity as they pass through the often turbulent teenage years. This goal won't be achieved if the social activities are swamped by non-Christians, and the norms and values of the group are destroyed.

This is just one example of how ineffective programming can cut across your goals, and the solution we have offered is just one solution. We *are not* saying that you must never have social nights out! We are saying that you must think about the place of socials in your program, and make sure that they are helping you achieve your goals.

3. The program was made for man, not man for the program

This is a truly liberating idea. Too many youth groups are enslaved by The Program. It runs rampant through the church like Godzilla through Tokyo.

Somewhere, sometime in the past, The Program was started by people who wished to accomplish something. It may have been ten years ago; it may have been last autumn. Chances are that when they set up The Program, things were in some way different from today. They may also have started with different goals in mind. It is quite possible that The Program has run its course and outlived its usefulness.

The person in charge of the youth ministry must realize that all programming is simply a tool by which the gospel is proclaimed. There is no intrinsic worth to the program. The program or fellowship group does not exist because there is some inherent value in keeping it going. Many churches have the view that they must continue certain ministries despite the cost and lack of results.

In other words, leaders must never be afraid of changing structures or bringing in new programs if they are convinced that these changes will prosper gospel ministry. It is a tragedy when the gospel suffers because of outdated methods or lack of initiative. One of the greatest hindrances to effective youth ministry is the famous line: "But we've always done it this way."

Remember, the program was made for man and not vice versa. If the various needs of the youth to whom you minister change or the program becomes outdated, either change your program, or suffer the consequences.

What about your group?

1. Does your current program resemble one of these three models?

2. In what areas is your program helping you achieve your goals?

3. In what areas is it hindering you?

4. What changes do you think need to be made to your program:

   • on the macro level?

   • on the micro level?

In search of the perfect haircut

Choosing youth leaders

"Things seem to be going very well in the youth program at the moment, Sean."

Sean Lamb and John Lansdowne were having their weekly staff meeting. The youth ministry at St Jason's seemed to be forging ahead. The numbers of young people attending Bible study groups had grown and Sean had added some new leaders to the team.

"I think one of the main reasons is the way I've been training our leaders. They've developed skills and confidence over time. Yeah, I'm pleased with it."

"Just one question, Sean. I noticed that you asked David to be the leader of one of your groups. Do you think that's wise?"

"Well, he's a very talented guy. He's doing engineering at Uni, he can play guitar, and the girls all love him. He seems to be able to attract the kids."

"But is he mature? He's only been a Christian for a few months. Don't you think you've thrown him in at the deep end?"

"Ah, well maybe. The real reason is that we're just desperate for leaders."

Who are our leaders?

It is certainly true of any group that it can only be as good as its leaders. The quality of leadership will have an enormous bearing on the quality of the group. This means that the way we go about choosing and training our leaders will be absolutely crucial.

So how do you do it? What kind of people should you be looking for to run your groups?

There is a temptation in youth ministry to choose leaders on the basis of their outward appearance. Indeed one could almost invent the identikit youth worker. He would have a radical haircut (i.e. very short, very long, or both at the same time), ear-rings, ride a motor-bike, look like Tom Cruise, play guitar like Eric Clapton, and play top grade football (you can work out the female equivalents). He'd be the coolest, strongest, funniest dude around. Of course, he or she would be great as a youth worker–surely all the kids would be attracted to him or her?

Now there is nothing inherently wrong with any of those things. Indeed, the authors of this book all bear an uncanny resemblance to Tom Cruise. But, funnily enough, that is never the way the Bible tells us to choose leaders. If you use superficial criteria, you will undoubtedly get superficial leaders.

It doesn't matter if you know who the latest big name musician is amongst the kids–what they really want to know is that you care for them.

What to look for

When Paul was writing to his young friend Timothy, and giving advice about who to choose as leaders, Paul told him to look on the inside. Paul's basis for selection was always the quality of a person's Christian life.

Look at 1 Timothy 3. Paul sets out what he thinks a leader of a group of Christians should be. Notice that he doesn't care very much about the way a person dresses. Paul *does* care about the way a leader treats other people (especially his family), his temper, and his attitude to money. A leader will not have a problem with alcohol, nor have a bad reputation. He will not be a recent convert, because having too much responsibility too soon may allow Satan to tempt him to pride.

Therefore, the basic principle when it comes to choosing leaders is to look for godliness first and gifts second.

There is a story about a man who was applying to become a missionary. The minister who was going to interview him told him to arrive at his house at 5 am. There was no public transport available, so the applicant got himself up at 3 am in the morning and walked. He rang the bell on arriving, and eventually the door was opened by the minister in his dressing gown. He ushered the young man in and told him to wait in the lobby while he had breakfast. An hour and a half later, the minister ushered the man into his study and sat him down for the interview.

"Do you love the Lord Jesus?" he asked.

"Yes sir, and with all my heart I want to serve him."

"Good. It's terribly important that you are well educated. Spell 'cat' for me". The young man did so.

"Excellent, now spell 'dog'." With mounting confusion, the young man complied.

"Now for arithmetic. What is 5+3?"

After a few more questions of this nature, the minister informed the young man that the interview had come to an end, thanked him for coming and sent him on his way.

Later that month when the committee met to decide on the application, the minister was confirmed in his opinion. The young man was accepted as a missionary, having been deemed to have demonstrated all the necessary qualities. He had shown discipline in making it to the interview on time, patience in waiting for the minister, and humility in never once pointing out what a farce the whole process was becoming. No time had been spent discussing the skills that might be needed in the mission field, but the crucial matter of the applicant's character had been established beyond all doubt.

Godliness first; gifts second. In a way, this sounds crazy. Surely we should be looking for really talented people to be our leaders.

However, if you think about it for a moment, you will see that godliness really is the key. There is nothing worse than working with someone who is extremely talented, but does not use those talents for the kingdom of God. If a person is self-centred, unreliable, evasive and deceitful, that person's ministry will not bring glory to God no matter how talented he or she is. The record of tele-evangelists in the US should have taught us these lessons—but sometimes we are slow to learn.

What are leaders for?

One of the interesting features about Paul's teaching on leadership is that he tells us more about who leaders *are* than what they *do*. This is because Paul understands what leadership is all about. Paul told his Thessalonian friends: "You know how we lived among you for your sake. You became imitators of us and of the Lord" (1 Thess 1:5-6).

The leader's most important task is to model the Christian life. Much of what we believe is caught and not taught. Many of us have modelled ourselves on more mature Christians, consciously or not. It doesn't matter if your leaders will be leading singing, leading Bible study groups, running games, or whatever. Leaders must be godly people, because they will be modelling the Christian life in everything they do.

The character of the leader will affect the character of the group. Over time, Christian groups become like their leaders—this is inevitable. The challenge for leaders, therefore, is to become the sort of people you want your group to become.

In the New Testament, being a leader is serious business:

- James says that leaders will have to give an account for the things they have taught (Jas 3:1).
- Peter tells us that we should lead because we want to, because it is our desire, not from any sense of obligation (1 Pet 5:1-4).
- Jesus teaches us that leadership is all about service. Leaders do not lord it over those for whom they are responsible. Leadership is serving; it is an act of love (Mk 10:35-45).

How to ask a leader

It is only fair when approaching someone to be involved in leadership that they know what they are in for. We must be totally up-front in identifying the responsibilities and tasks.

Ultimately, what is needed is a leadership team with gospel-centred priorities. And, interestingly enough, that will make the job of running the group much easier. If you have a group of keen people who see youth ministry as the expression of their ministry and the area in which they will exercise their gifts, then you won't have to flog them to do things. If youth work is seen as kingdom work, then the attendance of leaders at weekly meetings won't be in doubt. If you make the right choices at the beginning, your group will ultimately function more smoothly.

What does someone need to know before they join as a leader?

- The time of your big meeting each week. Presumably, attendance for leaders is compulsory. What are acceptable reasons for not attending? One group of leaders were told that if they missed more than three meetings a year, it would suggest that they weren't really serious.
- What is a leader's role in this meeting? Will they be preparing study material, or leading groups or games or singing? How much preparation will have to be done?
- When will the leaders meet with each other? How do people find out what is going on? When will the leaders be fed and encouraged? When will you pray for the group?
- What camps or other activities are planned during the year? Attendance will be compulsory at these.

Leaders kids love

Think about your teachers at school. Which ones did you like the best? Those who tried to be 'one of the kids' were despised. Those who were loved were firm and fair and showed that they loved you by teaching you well.

Youth leaders are not school teachers, and school teachers are not necessarily a model of what youth ministry is about. But there is something to be learned, nonetheless.

Knowing what fills up a kid's world can be a help in youth ministry. It can be an advantage to have an idea of the movies and TV they watch, the music they listen to and the sporting teams they follow.

But you cannot be 18 forever, so don't try. Young people do not need or want you to be another teenager. They need you to be a model of commitment to Christ. They need you to be someone who loves them because you know the love of Christ in your life.

As Paul says: "We loved you so much that we were delighted to share with you not only the gospel of God but our lives as well, because you had become so dear to us" (1 Thess 2:8).

Think about it

1. Read 1 Timothy 3 again. Compare your life and the ideal set out there. In what ways do you need to change?

2. Have you ever worked out a job specification for youth group leaders? Try to produce one that accurately sets out what leaders in your group should do.

3. Do you love the young people who come to your group? Do they know that you love them? What can you do about it?

4. Do you have any problems in the leadership of your group? How do you think they can be ironed out?

Multiplying yourself

Growing the ministry team

Ohne Friday night after youth group, Thommo looked at Jenny and said, "I've had enough. I'm resigning. I think I'm burnt out."

Thommo and Jenny had been youth leaders at Cedar Grove Baptist Church for three years. During that time their ministry had been quite successful. They had seen kids converted and grow as Christians, but the strain of running the group had finally got to them.

"Yeah, I want to resign too", Jenny replied. "But we can't. There's no-one to replace us. I keep on hoping that someone will turn up who can take our place, but no-one does. I think we're stuck with the job."

Thommo groaned. "You're right. I don't mind doing this, but as the group gets bigger, it just gets harder. What are we going to do?"

What is discipling?

The leader of any growing group quickly discovers one of the great problems of ministry. It is only possible to be close to a handful of people at any one time. This means that we can only have an impact on the lives of a very small number. The further we spread ourselves in trying to have regular contact, the thinner each contact becomes. It is possible to have a significant relationship only with about half a dozen people at any one time.

How then do we affect the lives of young people when a group grows beyond ten or twenty or thirty? The answer is that we must expand our ministry team. We must duplicate ourselves, so that others will have that same sort of impact. The process is one of multiplication.

When we tell someone the gospel and they respond, our job has only just begun. We must then work at helping them grow to Christian maturity. In this chapter, we shall look at the biblical concept of discipling—that is, prayerfully and faithfully building people up to be mature followers of the Lord Jesus. It is a vital part of good youth ministry, because it is the only way to overcome some of the problems experienced as the group grows. *Discipling is quite simply helping people to be disciples of Jesus.*

What does the Bible say about discipling?

Discipling includes the whole process of telling people the gospel, following them up and ensuring that they keep on growing as a Christian. In this sense, evangelism which stops short of discipling is bad evangelism. Evangelizing someone (i.e. 'gospelling' them) in one sense doesn't cease until the individual is mature in Christ. Colossians 1:28 says: "We proclaim him, admonishing and teaching everyone with all wisdom so that we may present everyone perfect in Christ".

All the New Testament letters are, in fact, follow-up letters. The initial evangelism had been done, but the gospel work continues as Paul now makes disciples through his letters. If you want to know what discipling is, read the letters of the New Testament.

Reading the Bible

1. Read Matthew 28:18-20. What does it say about discipling?

2. Look at these passages. What are new converts being taught?

- Romans 13:1-7

- 1 Corinthians 11:17-33

- 1 Corinthians 15:1-11

- Ephesians 5:22-6:9

- Colossians 4:2-6

Discipling and the youth leader

Every Christian needs to be discipled. However, discipling takes on a special importance for the youth leader. Only with an expanding ministry team can a youth group grow bigger than your individual gifts.

Like Thommo and Jenny, many youth leaders labour year after year on their own. Not only will they almost inevitably burn out, but they are limiting the group's growth.

You can ensure a steady stream of new, trained and motivated leaders by building a team of committed people who will work with you in this ministry and eventually be able to work independently of you.

To do this, you need to train leaders, but more than that you need to disciple them. It involves much more than just selecting someone who is keen and calling them a leader.

Discipling is moving people forward—in their knowledge of God; in their commitment to Christ; and in their commitment to serving others.

It involves pouring your life into a few key people. Note the example of the Lord Jesus—he chose twelve men and spent much of his time and energy preparing them for the work they were to do after his ascension.

It could have been different

Think about Thommo and Jenny's situation. It wasn't that there was an absolute lack of leadership potential within the group. The real problem was that no-one had done anything to develop that potential.

The situation could easily have been different. If Thommo had stopped and looked at his group, he would have seen that there was one of the older kids in particular who showed great promise. Dennis was serious about his commitment to Christ, was free of any hang-ups or great problems, and was keen to learn. He was a prime candidate to be discipled.

Let's imagine that Thommo asked Dennis to commit a couple of hours a week to meeting together so he could help Dennis grow as a Christian.

Over the next twelve months Dennis really did grow. When they met together, they talked about the Bible. They prayed. They read a book on leading a youth group. They shared their own personal struggles and triumphs as Christians. They went running together a couple of times a week. Over time, Thommo encouraged Dennis to take more and more responsibility in the group, at first organising games and then gradually building up to leading the Bible study.

At the end of the twelve months they were great mates. But more than that, Dennis was a much more mature follower of Jesus than he was before. In fact, now he was ready to meet with one of the younger blokes to help him grow.

In twelve months, Thommo would have expanded the ministry team by one. If Jenny had done the same with a female leader, the leadership team would have doubled. If in the next twelve months, all four discipled someone else, they would have grown to eight leaders in two years. Real life isn't always that perfect, but the point remains the same. Discipling produces real growth in a leadership team.

Whom should we disciple?

When looking for someone to disciple you should look for people who are FAT—i.e. Faithful, Available, Teachable.

* FAITHFUL: All the gifts and charisma in the world are of no value unless a person is faithful. You need to look for someone who is committed to the cause of Christ. They must be reliable—people who do as they promise, who turn up when they should and who see an obligation through to the end.
* AVAILABLE: To be a disciple, a person must be prepared to make time available. If the prospective disciple cannot find time amongst work, sport and leisure commitments to meet with you each week, then find someone else.
* TEACHABLE: The prospective disciple must be teachable. You are wasting your time with someone who thinks they already know it all.

When recruiting a potential disciple, it's important to give them a *vision* of the future, rather than simply an obligation to turn up. Be enthusiastic about the potential for Christian growth, for learning more, and for increased opportunities to serve others. Don't just sign up people for one hour per week. You are offering them the vision of much more.

Choose carefully, because you will be committing a lot of your life to this person. It is very difficult when things don't work out with someone you are discipling. In fact, it is often best to ask someone to meet with you for a set period of time; say 6 months. That way, if things don't work, you can finish the regular meetings without a feeling of failure.

Another hint: don't use the word 'disciple' when inviting someone to meet with you (as in, "How would you like to meet with me each week so that I can disciple you"). It sounds presumptuous, like you are full of yourself.

What do we do together?

What do we do together? When you meet together each week you might:

* Read the Bible
* Read books and articles together
* Work through a book like *The Blueprint*,[1] which deals with some basic theology
* Work on skills, such as how to give a Bible talk
* Pray together
* Review progress in the youth group
* Share future plans
* Go to the movies or the beach
* Use your imagination—share your life with these people.

Dream and scheme together. Be open about what you are planning to do. Your aim should be to get the disciple to a stage where he or she can train others.

This can only be done with a couple of people at a time. You can't disciple fifty people at once. If you can train one person to work alongside you and to evangelize and disciple others, then you have doubled your effectiveness.

The person not the program

Ministry is about people, not about building organizations or programs. So too in discipling—we must be concerned for the whole person. We must be committed to doing what is best for each individual, not just fitting them into the structure.

As you try to expand your ministry team, it is important to remember that you must take each person's gifts and personality into account. To give someone a job for which they are not suited is a recipe for disaster. We must always suit the job to the person, rather than trying to make the person fit the job.

As you train disciples, you will gradually involve them in

1. Available from Matthias Media.

more and more ministry, and train them on the job. As they grow, you encourage them to begin training others. Eventually, you may see less of them as they become busy in ministry to others. Thus the process is repeated.

A word of warning

If you're going to disciple someone, make sure it is someone of the same sex. To get this close to someone of the opposite sex has potential for disaster. Do not do it!

We must not only do what is right in male/female relationships, we must also be seen to do the right thing (Eph 5:3). This is such an important topic, we've devoted a whole chapter to it (Chapter 11, "Confessions of a Youth Leader").

Recommended reading: *Disciples are Made not Born*, Walter Hendriksen (Navigator Press, 1989)

Think about it

1. Who are the people who have had the biggest impact on your Christian life? How have they done this?

2. Who do you know that is FAT? You probably won't use the word 'disciple', but how could you go about establishing this sort of relationship with someone?

Flat out like lizards

A strategy for evangelism

"I'm just not sure that we're going about it the right way."

John Lansdowne, the senior pastor, and Sean Lamb, the youth worker, were discussing evangelism. Sean was speaking.

"I know we've seen people converted in the last 12 months, but most of that has been through what you and I have done. I sometimes feel like we're the only people who are interested in evangelism."

"Well, I don't think that's true, but I share your feelings. I think people would like to tell their friends about Jesus, but they don't know how to do it. The problem is, I'm not sure what we can do."

"We'd better think of something", said Sean. "There are a lot of people out there we're never going to reach if it's just up to you and me."

Frogs and lizards

At a recent international conference on Evangelism, a speaker asked the question, "Who are the best evangelists?" He then went on to explain differences in the eating habits of frogs and lizards!

Think about it for a moment. A frog likes to eat flies and other insects. Frogs are not very mobile creatures, so their best approach is to remain perfectly still and wait till their prey comes to them. When an insect flies by, they pounce. Then they wait until another passes.

A lizard, on the other hand, is more active in tracking down its food. It is mobile and able to chase its prey. It can get out in the jungle amongst the other animals and find what it wants.

The point of the comparison is this: those people involved in full-time Christian work are like frogs–they wait for non-Christians to come to them. They don't have contacts at work or at school. The opportunities that come their way tend to be more formal or structured, like wedding or baptism interviews, or people visiting church.

People who work or go to school or Uni or college are like lizards. They are in a much better position to meet non-Christians and evangelize them. They are out in the jungle, where the good opportunities are. Who is in the best position for evangelism? It is the lizards and not the frogs.

The aim of youth evangelism

What is evangelism? It's people who know the good news about Jesus telling other people who don't. Good youth evangelism enables this to happen by training young people to evangelize their friends. They will ultimately be the most effective evangelists–they have the opportunities, the relationships and the credibility.

The task of the leaders, then, is to train and equip young people for evangelism. A good youth program will also provide evangelistic meetings that are not embarrassing, to which the group members can confidently bring their friends.

Training in evangelism should be a high priority in your youth program. It will need to include three different aspects:

- Motivation to evangelism
- Skills in evangelism
- Confidence in evangelism

People will be motivated to evangelize when they realise that it is the whole thrust of the Bible. God's purposes on earth are worked out as we proclaim the kingdom and see people come under the Lordship of Christ. The Bible envisages people being trained to do this, as in Ephesians 4 where Paul describes the work of preparing God's people to do good works in the name of Christ. And if our young people are motivated and well-trained, they will have confidence to share the gospel with their friends. Then we will begin to see the gospel growing in our community.

How to produce a group of lizards

The best things in life often start small. The way to produce a group of evangelistically minded young people is to train them well. Start off by choosing a small group of soundly converted people with potential for evangelism. Whatever you do, don't call for volunteers—you might get some! Select people carefully. If others want to do the course, explain that you will be running it again as soon as this one ends, and they can join then.

After you have selected, then invite. Write a letter which outlines the things involved in the course. Letters are help-ful because they suggest a certain formality and seriousness about the exercise. By putting the proposal in writing, we give people time to consider their response. It is important to set out completely all that is involved so that there are no hidden costs, time requirements or expectations. (We've included a sample letter at the end of this chapter.)

When the group meets, use the time to teach an evangelis-tic tool. *Two Ways To Live* (available from Matthias Media) is a good summary of the gospel that can be presented in a few minutes. The training course provides heaps of information about what evangelism is and how to do it.

The great advantage of this approach to training is that you will be teaching successive groups of lizards. If the leader of the group is the only evangelist, then there is a limit to the number of people he or she can reach. But if you teach eight other people to be evangelists, you have greatly multiplied the possibilities for evangelism.

You will need to show people how to evangelize in person. Use the time in the training groups to teach the Bible's perspective on evangelism, to pray for each other and your gospel contacts, and to encourage one another to be faithful witnesses.

A process not an event

Sometimes we expect to see the fruit of evangelism too soon, or we forget that most non-Christian people need time to evaluate and decide how to respond to the challenge we are presenting.

Evangelism is a process not an event. It takes time to become a Christian. People often need to hear the gospel explained six or seven times before the message gets through. The whole process quite often takes a year or more.

Therefore, we need to make sure that our whole program is evangelistic. It is not enough to have one or two gospel events or talks in a year. We have to be certain that the meetings we run are attractive to outsiders.

While there will always be a tension between activities that will stretch maturing Christians and those that will appeal to the unconverted, we need to avoid leaning too far in one direction or the other.

Our youth meetings need to be seen through the eye of an outsider. What does it feel like to come for the first time? If it's not pleasant, then it's unlikely that people will come back. We need to be sure that the meeting is well-organized. There must be no intimidation or hassling of other members. This is always a problem in groups. Young people love to insult each other for a joke, and sometimes they overstep the mark. They can be both extremely cruel to each other, and yet incredibly sensitive about what others say. Creating an atmosphere of respect and trust is vital to growing a group. As has been discussed earlier, setting a group norm is essential so that outsiders who come conform to it, and not vice versa.

It is also worth considering how outsiders are welcomed

into our groups. Despite best intentions, Christian groups can be extremely unfriendly to the outsider. Cliques based around peer networks often exclude those who don't belong to the right circles or go to the right schools.

When people join a group, the group dynamics will change. One reason some groups stay small is that people like it that way (whether they are conscious of it or not). Growth often means pain; it means the loss of a small and comfortable atmosphere.

Youth evangelism and church

Ultimately, our aim is to see young people develop into mature Christians. This will necessarily mean encouraging them to join with other Christians to be edified and encouraged. One of the important steps to maturity is regular attendance at church.

The normal time for young people to go to church in our culture is Sunday night. The evening services in many churches are seen as the 'youth services', aimed at the younger members of the congregation. Often these services will have an evangelistic thrust from time to time.

Of course, what happens in church services will often be out of the hands of the youth leader. Nevertheless, as much as we are able, we should still aim to have church services that are as attractive as possible to the outsider. This will mean thinking about the type of language used, singing, notices and drama. We also need to be careful about what is preached and how. If the sermon is incomprehensible, why would you want to come back?

Summing up

Effective youth evangelism will happen when we train our young people to be effective evangelists. We should consider carefully how evangelism fits into the overall framework of our group, so that our activities are genuinely attractive to the outsider.

Use the questions below to think about how your group is going with evangelism.

What about your group?

1. How would you describe the evanglistic strategy that your youth group has at the moment? How could it be improved?

2. Is your group friendly to outsiders?

3. What opportunities does your group provide for outsiders to be invited?

4. How could you begin to train evangelists in your group?

Example of a letter written to begin an evangelism training group.

Dear Carolynne,

It might seem a little strange for me to be writing to you when I see you so often, but I want to give you an invitation. The reason I'm writing to you is that I'm not able to make this offer to everyone in the youth group.

One of the important jobs given to Christian leaders in the Bible is to help equip other Christians so they can do the work of ministry (Ephesians 4:11-12). One of the most important things that we can do as Christians is to share the Gospel with other people. I would like to try to help you do that better. I'd like to help you have the confidence to speak to people about Jesus.

I'm planning to run a group at the church on Friday nights. I expect the group would run from about 7:30 until 10:00 pm. Over seven meetings I'd like to take you and a few others through a course on evangelism that teaches you how to use the little booklet 2 Ways to Live. We'll learn what the Bible says about evangelism, how to use 2 Ways to Live, how to answer questions we get asked, and we'll pray for our non-Christian friends.

I think this could be a really great time together, but we need to be committed to the group and to attending each session unless there's a good reason. The dates of the seven Friday nights are listed below. The workbook for the course costs $15.00.

I have listed the dates of our meetings and the names of the other people who I've invited to do the course on the attached sheet of paper. Please don't talk about this with anyone not on the list. It's not that this is an elitist thing, but I couldn't invite everyone to come along. Have a think about it and let me know—don't feel under any obligation. If you do decide that you'd like to be involved, please let me know by Wednesday, 14 March. As usual, if you've got any questions please ring me.

Yours sincerely,
Sean Lamb

Friends and foes

Parents, discipline and games

Parents

"Annabel, we've got a problem."

John Lansdowne sounded somewhat apologetic. "You know I think you and the other leaders do a wonderful job, but we have received a number of complaints."

Annabel looked surprised. "Complaints. What about?"

"About the last outing actually. It seems that the kids were supposed to be back at 10.00, but they didn't arrive till 11.00. The parents were concerned because they didn't know where their children were. Did you send home a note?"

"Well, no. We often do, but we didn't get around to it."

"Do you know many of the parents?"

"Umm, a few who come to church."

"You know, it may not be a bad public relations exercise if you visited them. They might be a little more forgiving the next time you bring their kids home late."

Parents and the youth leader

Parents are a vital link in the youth ministry chain. After all, they are the ones who have the kids. And believe it or not, in most cases they actually love them.

Consequently, it's important to get to know the parents of the children for whom you are responsible. They are usually concerned about who is running the group that their child attends. It will also give you some idea of the environment which the kids have grown up in, thus enabling you to minister more effectively.

During your time with parents, you can talk about the

activities that you run as part of the group, future events that you are planning, and how their child relates with others. You could also ask if they have any particular concerns about their child, and if there is any way in which you can help.

Parents are almost always positive when you visit. Even if they are not Christians, they will at least appreciate the time and effort that you spend caring for their son or daughter. As a youth leader, you are providing child care and education free of charge to the parent and at considerable cost to yourself. There is no need to feel embarrassed about what you do with the group.

However, we need to be sensitive about who does the visiting. It is better to have the parents visited by a leader of the same sex as their teenager, or by a leader who is at least much older. We don't want to give them the wrong idea!

So, visit parents! Even a visit once every few months is enough to keep up a good relationship. The obvious place to start is with parents already associated with the church.

Part of the reason why visiting is so important is that openness and transparency must mark what you do at the youth group. Non-Christian parents can get rightly worried about their son or daughter 'getting religion'. Fears about intense sects are only exacerbated if there is any sense of secrecy about what is going on. They need to be reassured that you are trustworthy as far as their child is concerned. Try to communicate regularly with parents, and make it clear exactly what you are doing with their precious child. Publish the aims of your group on the programme, and maybe even schedule the occasional parents evening. One group once ran the entire parents evening as though it was a regular youth group—with singing, crazy games, and a serious Bible talk on the responsibilities of parents—while their kids were in the next room having a talk on honouring their parents!

Honouring parents

Speaking of honouring parents, it is important to teach the children in your youth group proper respect and obedience toward their parents (see Eph 6:1 and Ex 20:12). Regardless of whether the parents are Christian or not, it is important that parents be treated in the right way—children should do this because it is the right thing to do. If they do not treat their parents properly, it will completely undermine any Christian witness they are trying to have at home.

There may be genuine difficulties when non-Christian parents make it hard for their Christian sons or daughters to come to church or youth group. We must pray hard and look for alternatives to having them directly disobey or confront their parents. It may be possible to have the need for Christian fellowship met in some other way—for example, in Christian groups at school, or with other members of the youth group who are fellow students. While the child lives at home, every effort must be made to live in honour and obedience to their parents, up to the point where it would mean disobeying God. Even after leaving home, we must still treat our parents with love and respect.

Parents and conflict

The overwhelming reaction of most parents is gratitude and enthusiasm for the work that youth leaders do. They are very thankful and appreciative of the time and effort poured into the lives of their teenagers. Teenage years are often difficult for the teenagers themselves as they make the transition from children to adults, but they can also be very painful years for the parents of these children as they become adults. There are difficulties in communication, especially about the most significant things like their Christian faith, and it is in these difficult years that youth group leaders can make such a difference.

Given this sense of gratitude from parents, why is there

sometimes conflict between parents and youth leaders? Strangely enough, conflict between parents and youth group leaders usually takes place between Christian parents and youth group leaders rather than non-Christian parents and youth group leaders. The non-Christian parents seem to have less expectations about youth groups and are generally happy for anything that's done for their teenagers. Christian parents however, have higher expectations of what should happen and are much more emotionally involved about the Christian commitment of their teenagers.

There are two main causes for conflict between parents and youth leaders. One cause of conflict comes when, despite everyone's efforts, the teenager decides to walk away from Christ and loses interest in church and youth group. This walking away from the Christian faith can lead to despair, frustration, bewilderment and heart-break on the part of parents. They can feel powerless and uncertain what to do, and unfortunately will often look around for someone or something to blame. They may blame the leaders, the program, the particular teaching, the style and feel of the group, or all of the above. Sometimes even the most faithful of Christian parents will be inclined to suggest that the Christian content of a group should be downplayed in order to make the group more fun to attend. This can lead to difficult situations where parents are pushing one way for the sake of their children (as they see it), and youth leaders hold the line of needing to teach the Bible. Great wisdom is called for in these situations and it's often a good idea to involve someone older in the church who is able to speak to parents as a peer. This may be a time to involve the senior pastors of the church.

Sometimes, the parents are right—the program is too stifling, with nothing but dead-serious Bible study. Teenagers do need to have fun, relax and just blow off some steam. We need to make sure that we allow time for both sorts of activities in our program—for making disciples of Christ through prayerful Bible teaching; and for just having fun and being Christian friends together.

Conflict can also arise when parents are pushing their teen-agers to achieve academically, musically, on the sporting field, and so on. Unfortunately, it is sometimes Christian parents who tell their teenagers that they do not have time for proper involvement in Christian activities, because they need to be studying, learning music, training for sport, or whatever it is. This reflects a problem with the Christian life of the parents rather than the teenagers; it is what we want for our children that really reflects our values in life. Once again, great wisdom is needed here as youth leaders discuss with parents the time allocation and priorities of their teenagers. It is also suggested that older members of the church be involved to discuss things with parents as peers, and this is a good time to involve the senior pastors or elders of the church to gently discuss this matter.

Discipline

Tanglebank Presbyterian is not far from St Jason's. It has a thriving youth ministry, with an energetic and apparently successful youth worker. Many adults in the congregation are delighted to see the evening service full to overflowing.

However, the minister, David Hedges, did not share their enthusiasm. In fact, he found the evening service to be a real chore. While there might have been masses of young people in attendance, he wondered about their real motives for coming along. There was a large section of high schoolers who sat in the back few rows each week and talked incessantly throughout the service. Even the prayer time was not immune from the constant drone of juvenile voices.

One night, Rev. Hedges finally blew a fuse and unleashed his anger during the sermon. Raising his voice, he railed at many of the young people, telling them that they must reassess their motives for coming to church each week. He demanded a change in behaviour. Most of the kids just stared at the floor thinking, "Who is this jerk?"

After the service, when everyone had gone, the youth worker challenged David Hedges in a frustrated voice. "You have just undone all that I have worked for in getting these kids to church. Many of them would never have darkened the doors of the church if it hadn't been for my efforts in making them feel comfortable and unthreatened. You have just set my work back by months!"

In many churches today, the evening service is considered to be the youth service. Often it is counted a real victory when kids are in the church building, with the unstated assumption that discipleship takes place through osmosis. In some churches, it even appears that the philosophy of spiritual growth is that if the kids will sit there week after week, the Holy Spirit will be able to operate through the clamour and transform them into disciples.

Many churches have set out with the noble goal of getting unchurched kids into church, and making church as non-threatening as possible. While they may have been successful in this, the side effect is often similar to Tanglebank Presbyterian. What are the problems with this approach?

1. While it is great to get unchurched kids to attend church, if your goal is just to get them to sit there, you cannot help but create false expectations. Many of the young people will think that somehow just 'being there' is what it is all about. They will resign themselves to 'toughing it out' for the duration of the service so that they can enjoy the social interaction afterwards. The church service is relegated to being a ritual or penance.

2. By letting the kids know that it is acceptable to talk all the way through the service, pass notes, eat, and even get up and walk out, the youth leader is communicating many things. He is saying, in effect, that what is going on in church is not really important enough to listen to. If the message of the gospel is the most important message in the world, then this is a tragedy. The young people regard what takes place in the service as

unimportant because this is what the youth leader has communicated to them by the behavioural standards he has set.

3. The people who do listen present another problem. They do regard church as important, but are prevented from fully concentrating due to the constant rabble in the background.

4. Once a 'non-threatening' norm is set up in a youth service, it is quite hard to change. When the kids are out of order and discipline is necessary, the discipline comes as a shock and seems out of place. The person administering the discipline automatically becomes an ogre.

5. Finally, we must remember that the gospel calls for a radical change of behaviour affecting every aspect of life. If and when the young people actually listen and hear this, the threatening nature of the gospel will not fit with their experience.

The way forward

While it is good to have evening church meetings pulsating with young people, it is more important to have evening meetings thriving with disciples. Any event that the church runs—from the Christmas party to the week-by-week evening meeting—must promote Christian growth. It is simply not helpful to allow our meetings to descend into chaos. Young people need to grow in a loving but disciplined environment where the claims of the gospel can be heard. It is a myth that kids will not respond well to discipline. The most loving thing a youth worker can do is show the young people that God is serious and that his people are serious about listening to him.

If the problem kids are from church families, the discipline problem should be politely referred back to their parents—another reason why a good relationship with parents is a great help.

For those kids who aren't from Christian families, the

problem is more difficult. It may be necessary to prevent these kids attending for a time if they are disrupting the event for everyone else.

Whatever you do, remember the principle: praise in public, discipline in private. If someone gets in trouble and you have to speak to them, do it privately; allow them to maintain their dignity.

What about your group?

1. What are the standards you feel that your church has set regarding behaviour in the evening service?

2. Is behaviour a problem in your church?

3. What steps, if any, would you take to discipline kids?

4. Reflect on 1 Corinthians 14:33 and Hebrews 12:11. What light do these verses shed on the subject of discipline and church?

Games

Imagine if you will, that someone were to offer you a programming device that would in one fell swoop grant you these exciting options:

- it would take up a lot of time, making your program full
- it would create an atmosphere of joy and exuberance
- it would allow the kids a time to mix
- it would provide an opportunity for raucous young people to expend some of their boundless stores of energy.

Does this sound too good to be true? Of course not, because almost every youth group in Australia already devotes a substantial amount of time to the part of their program called 'games'. Games may vary in content and intensity but it might be true to say that *Streets & Lanes* and *Honey, if you love me smile* are part of the Christian subculture.

One characteristic of almost every young person (and old person for that matter) is that while they may outwardly groan and say "not this game again", inwardly they love games. They love the atmosphere games bring. They love the heat of battle. And young people relish the opportunities games provide to mingle and mix (i.e. get to know the opposite sex).

While games promise much, they have a 'flip-side'—there is an element of danger involved in devoting a large segment of your program to them. Have games ceased being our friend and become our foe?

For many youth groups, using games in a program is like buying a puppy–great fun and lovely to begin with, but when it turns out to be a Great Dane, it eats you out of house and home, and is impossible to control.

Our major concern with games is this: despite their inherent attractiveness, they also constitute a danger–that the 'game time' will assume primary importance. Youth group members may 'put up with' the other parts of the program because the games are so much fun. An unnecessary dependency on games begins to creep in. The kids enjoy them and the leaders feel good because the youth group may be growing.

It must be stated that *good games do not equal a good program.* If your aim is to evangelize young people and then disciple them to be like Christ, then your program must reflect this in every aspect. It is very easy to divert the undisciplined mind of a young person away from Christ to the joys and intricacies of *British Bulldog.* We are not saying that games must be done away with altogether. But like all elements of a program, the games must fit in, have a purpose, and accomplish the goals you set for them.

Allow us to offer some helpful hints.

- Games must facilitate the more important side of your program. If you need games to fill up the program, you may need to change the program! Our task is to make disciples, and playing *Stuck in the Mud* may not be the most effective way of achieving this. On the positive side, games can be used to accomplish many things, such as crowd breaking and helping reticent kids to mingle. They can help build a sense of team spirit and achievement, as well as a sense of history ('remember when...'). And of course, games also can release pent up energy. The thinking leader must scrutinize his program carefully and make sure that the games do this without detracting from the other more important aspects.

* Games should have a flow. This simple idea is often ignored. If games are a necessary part of your program, then use your brain—begin with the rowdy 'race around and exert energy' games, and then run a game that's a bit less rowdy, and then another that is quieter still, and so on. Instead of going into the next part of the program high as kites, the kids have been brought down to earth. The next segment of your program should be a 'bridge', such as announcements, to allow a final settling down time.

* Make the games relational. Games can often do much in the way of breaking down barriers, getting a group to relate to one another, and bonding a group together. If this is your goal, you must pay careful attention to the content of your games. There is certainly a place for those games which allow the kids to run, scream and generally cause pandemonium. Yet games can also allow them to relate to each other in a way they may not be able to in school or in the secular world.

* An example of a good 'relational' game—there is a circle of seats facing outward with a corresponding number of seats in an outer circle facing inward. The group is seated so that everyone is facing another member of the group. The leader then asks a series of questions. After each question the people facing each other must introduce themselves and then in turn answer the question. When enough time has elapsed, the leader then tells the group to relocate, e.g. "Those sitting in the outside circle must move three seats to the right". The leader then asks a new question. As the game progresses, the questions become more and more serious (you can relate some of the questions to the forthcoming talk/ Bible study).

What about your group?

1. Review your program and rate the place of games in your program in terms of a scale of 1 to 10.

1 ——————————————— 5 ——————————————— 10

"Games?! Our two hour
program is taken up
with a verse by verse
exposition of
Deuteronomy."

"The ten minutes
we devote to
serious things are
squeezed in between
games of Fruit Salad
and Poison Ball."

2. Do games have a different role in your various meetings each week?

3. Think about what would happen to your program if games were either dropped out or their importance was lessened.

4. Think about what you are trying to achieve with your games component. Are you achieving your goals? Would you be better off focusing your efforts elsewhere?

Mountain-top experiences

Making the most of camps

10

It was only the next morning that the youth camp leaders discovered what had really happened after midnight. Of course, they were the ones who'd gone to bed promptly at 11 pm, knowing they'd have to be up early to prepare their Bible studies. They'd said good night to the young people sitting round the camp fire and thought they'd received promises that everyone would be asleep in their tents pretty soon.

The next day they found out that some of the teenagers hadn't gone to bed at all. Some had gone for a middle-of-the-night hike (where they'd had to shrug off the attractions of someone who seemed intent on following them); another took his motorbike down onto the beach and then went for a swim. Most of them, however, just hung around the camp fire talking and telling stories into the early hours.

The leaders were disappointed, but glad everyone seemed to be having an OK time. They did think it was a shame, however, that so many were late for breakfast and then chose to lie down during the Bible studies. And they did begin to worry more about what would be reported back to the church and to parents.

Over the years, the fellowship camp (or 'houseparty' or 'weekend away' or whatever your group calls it) has become an integral part of most youth programs. In many cases, it has become a tradition, and there is little thought put into why the camp is actually taking place. Each year, like a change in the seasons, the annual camp just rolls around.

Why do some camps reach great heights while others just limp along? It may be that the leaders have not stopped to ask themselves the all-important question: Why are we having this camp?

Why have a camp?

1. It's a unique gospel opportunity

There's you, a bunch of young people and lots of time, amidst all the other activities, to teach them the gospel of Jesus clearly and engagingly. It's likely that time always feels limited in your week by week youth ministry. Camps provide a longer opportunity to teach the Bible well and explain the gospel.

That won't mean longer meetings: it will mean better use of the meetings over the whole camp. You can also think how you can bring a fresh, less predictable approach to those meetings.

It's likely that the new environment will help as well: being away from home (and homework and parents) gives young people a chance to think more carefully about what they're being taught in the youth group back home and what it means to them. It may also be the case that an 'outside' speaker will be able to reap where you have sown: he or she may say exactly what you've been saying for weeks, but it could just sink in when it comes with a fresh voice. Many people look back and say that it was on camp as a young person that they took significant steps forward with Christ.

2. It's a life-to-life situation

Spending 48 or more hours in the company of young people provides a great opportunity for you to model the Christian life to them. It's not a case of performing or showing off, simply a matter of letting your life show what it is to follow Christ daily. After all, they'll see you as you get up in the morning, as you lead a Bible study, as you chat over meals, as you play a game, as you react when you get tired. It's worth thinking what your behaviour on camp would teach others:

are you being a good model to follow? Does your manner of life point people to Christ?

This has implications for the way leaders relate to each other over the camp: is there a battle to be the coolest, wittiest and best at everything? Or are the young people seeing us serve each other, build each other up and enjoy each other's company?

3. It's a good time to build friendships

It's often the case that, week by week, youth leaders are so busy putting chairs out, preparing an activity, sorting out troublemakers and looking out for newcomers that they fail to ask any of their young people any question at all.

Camps are a chance to rectify that situation. Leaders need to take the opportunity to sit, listen and talk with their teenagers—about anything and everything. We need to learn how to get beyond asking: 'So, how's school, then?' The best way to do that is to spend time in their company, taking an interest in their lives. Meal times can be great for this.

For the leader, of course, this personal work is essential if we're to teach the gospel well and help young people turn to Christ and then grow as Christians. Good youth ministry is always relational: so get to know your young people as individuals. Where you have a team of leaders, you can work together at ensuring no teenager gets neglected.

4. It's a chance to build the group

Camps have a habit of living long in the youth group's memory: The 'Do you remember when Ronnie…?' story will be revisited several years after the event. Make the most of this by making camp fun. Do crazy new things they haven't done before, find activities that stretch and intrigue them, make sure you do several activities as a whole group together.

Camp also provides a chance to break down some of the group's cliques and to settle in newcomers. Work at mixing people well.

5. It enables growth in leadership

Camp provides lots of moments for training and growing your leaders. Younger leaders can be given up-front responsibilities that may not be possible week-by-week: giving notices, saying a brief testimony, overseeing a washing up team, and so on.

They should be able to see an older leader modelling how a task is done well and then do likewise. Younger leaders will learn from watching how older leaders build friendships, lead Bible studies, use 'dead' time, run activities, referee games, sort out trouble spots, pray in leaders' meetings and anticipate what's ahead. This will help train younger leaders that Christian ministry involves service, not limelight-hunting.

A practical guide to camps

Having been convinced that a thoughtfully prepared camp is just what your group needs, you now set out to prepare one for your youth group. How is this done? There are six key ingredients:

The speaker and the talks
The theme
Group work
Meal times
Free time
The site

1. The speaker and the talks

Assuming that you are planning a camp where the Bible is going to be taught, it is crucial that the Bible is taught well. Consider the following points when planning this aspect of your camp:

- Select your speaker carefully—he should further your cause, but unless you are careful he may do just the opposite! Camps are not the time to break in new speakers or let just anyone have a go. Speakers must be screened carefully–they must be people that you trust, whom you know will teach the Bible to your group in a way that they will understand. (Of course, you can also choose to handle the Bible talks among your own leadership team. This has the advantage of guaranteeing reliability and unity of message. However, it has two disadvantages–you lose the sense of dynamism and freshness brought by a different voice; and it doubles the amount of work required to organize the camp!)

- Once you have found a speaker, do not ask him simply to speak on 'anything he wants to'. If he is a regular camp speaker, he will probably have several talks up his sleeve. You can either see if one of his talks fits into your goals for the camp, or ask him to write new talks for the occasion.

- Make sure that you communicate your goals for the camp to the speaker. Be specific. For example, if the camp is to be evangelistic, make sure that the speaker realizes there will be non-Christians there. It may be helpful for the speaker to meet the camp leaders once or twice before the weekend so that he can tailor the talks to the needs of the group, and so that the leaders can prepare suitable group discussion questions (if these are to be used).

2. The theme

A theme helps you to promote a camp, as well as aiding the learning process on the weekend itself. Having a theme builds awareness. If you advertise imaginatively (and often) the group members will have the topic in their heads even before they get to the camp. Focused promotion makes the camp seem like an event, rather than just another weekend away together. Your imagination is the only limit to the number of ways you can develop the theme of the camp both before and during the weekend.

3. Small groups

Small groups can play a very significant part in your camp—if you use them well. Small groups allow you to mix the kids up. They provide an opportunity for forming new friendships and sharing with each other in a comfortable setting. While most camps have standard 'discussion groups' after the talk, the imaginative leader can use small groups in a variety of ways. For example:

- *Electives*. On Saturday night, offer a number of topics to be discussed in small groups. Each group is run by a prepared leader, and there is time left for discussion. Topics could include prayer, evangelism, what a Christian is, Christians and parties, etc. The list is endless.
- *Prayer groups*. Divide the camp up into small groups (of 4–5) and set a time aside for them to pray for the needs of the group and the camp.

4. Free time

It is a common myth that unstructured free time is the high point of the camp for the young people. Very few of your campers will look back on the free time as the highlight of the weekend. The wise camp leader will strike a balance between too much free time and too little. If you are following the typical pattern of lunch, free time, and then a late afternoon talk, it is probably best to schedule a compulsory (and enjoyable!) activity after lunch for an hour or so. (Campsite directors can often help with activities if you organize it with them in advance.) Then make sure you allow a few hours of unstructured time to let the kids burn off some energy.

5. Meal times

Meal times are awaited with eager anticipation by the campers, but they are often overlooked by the leaders as a ministry opportunity. Perhaps you thought meal times were just for eating—not so! Like any other aspect of your camp, you can make meal times work for you in achieving your goals. Here are a few possibilities:

- Meal times are a great opportunity to 'break in' people who have shown up-front leadership potential. You can get them to organize the orderlies, say grace, oversee the distribution of the food, explain the next part of the program, and so on.
- 'Mini-testimonies' or devotionals also fit in well at meal times. They don't have to be anything long or heavy—just a 3–to–5 minute spot for someone to share what they've learned recently, or how they became a Christian.
- Meals can be used as time for prayer around the tables.
- If there has been an emphasis on small groups at the camp, have the groups sit together during one of the meals just to be together socially. You can also have each small group present a skit to provide some comic relief.

6. The site

Of course, you also need to find the right site for your camp, in terms of location, cost, number of campers, activities, meeting rooms, and so on. This is one aspect of camp planning that needs to be done a long way in advance—up to a year if possible. Think carefully about all the different factors, and what would be best for the whole group—not what you yourself would prefer, and not necessarily the time-honoured location for the past 10 years.

Once you have these six essential components worked out, you are well on the way to a fantastic, learning, growing, life-changing weekend! There are some other tips we'd like to give you on good camp management. Even if you have all the above ingredients right, there is another factor that can make the difference between a mediocre weekend and a memorable one. That difference is you—the leader.

Think about it

1. What was the best camp you've even been on? What made it so successful?

2. What was the worst camp you've ever been on? Why was it such a flop?

3. Think about your most recent fellowship camp. Did the camp have any clear goals? Were they achieved?

4. How could a camp contribute to the goals you now have for your group?

Some tips for good camp leading

1. Be organized

As you have been reading this chapter, you will have no doubt realized that running a good camp takes a lot of effort. It almost goes without saying that you have to be *organized* in advance to have any hope of making the most of your camp. There are a hundred things that can go wrong on a camp and ninety-nine of them can usually be prevented through preparation. The well-prepared leader will have thought through every aspect of the camp—pencils, sporting equipment, a music player for the dance, bringing extra Bibles, and so on. The well-prepared leader will also make sure that everything is communicated clearly to kids and their parents—what to bring, where to go, arrival and departure times, and so on.

Teenagers respond to a sense of purpose and direction. If you know what you are doing and what is happening next, and are able to communicate that to the campers, you will find them more than willing to follow your lead.

2. Be flexible and spontaneous

Contrary to first appearances, this is not in direct opposition to the first rule! Even the best laid plans sometimes need modification. Always keep in mind your goals for the camp, and if you find that some of them are being achieved spontaneously, then go with the flow. For example, the Saturday morning speaker has just given a challenging message on building each other up. At morning tea, you observe quite a number of people seeking to restore broken relationships. It would be madness to rush on to the next activity and break this up—it would be better to let morning tea run on for an extra 20 minutes and make up the time later.

3. Have one main leader

A camp will not work as a democracy. This may sound like a threat to the Constitution, but it is true. One person must be the ultimate authority and be seen by all to be The Leader. He or she may choose to share the leadership with a team, but ultimately one person needs to take responsibility for what happens on the weekend. Needless to say, this job must be given to the right person—a lack of wise, decisive leadership has ruined many a camp.

4. Be observant

The Camp Leader is in many ways the lynch-pin of a successful camp (the speaker runs a close second). The Leader must always keep a watchful eye on the teenagers, the other leaders, the mood, the program, the amount of sleep, discipline, the camp site, the weather, the cooks, the speaker, and his own sanity. He must notice everything and make sure that the program is doing what it is supposed to do—i.e. meeting its goals. This takes time and lots of practice.

5. Stay in control

One of the most difficult issues a leader will have to face is discipline. How late do you let the kids stay up and what do you do if they just will not go to bed? What do you do when you find a camper with alcohol?

The wise leader maintains a balance between excessive discipline and total freedom. Take, for instance, the young people who refuse to go to sleep. Every camp leader has experienced this problem. It will usually take three or four visits before they will settle down. The leader must show them that he is reasonable—that he will let them stay awake for a time. But he must also show them that he will not budge when they have reached the deadline. He must be seen to be serious and in control, even if it means removing some of the noise-makers from the room, or standing outside their door until he is sure they are asleep. Never be tempted to let the campers rule the roost. It will wreck the weekend for everybody.

6. Have a good time

Enjoy the weekend that you have organized and are running!

Camps operate better when the leaders are not hassled and stressed. The weekend you have planned will probably be used by God to bring about some change in a young person's life. Feel privileged that God has allowed you to be involved in this ministry. Even if everything seems to have gone wrong, we have a Father who works out all things in accordance with his will, and works in all things for good. He can turn a disaster into a miracle.

Confessions of a youth leader

Sex in your youth group

11

"The talk had been a minor personal triumph. I had presented the Biblical teaching on marriage and sex with clarity and power. Now I was basking in the feedback as one of the most attractive girls explained why the talk had been so helpful to her personally. My earnest concentration on her every word made it clear to everyone else that I was not to be disturbed. It's times like these, when the adrenalin is pumping, that ministry is more like a game than hard work."

Where there is smoke...

The problem is that ministry is no game—especially when sexual attraction begins to play a part.

Each year, a number of ministers and youth leaders make ship-wreck of their lives and ministries through sexual sin. Some don't get found out; some suddenly disappear as everything is discreetly covered up; and some even end up facing criminal charges.

We are not just talking about twisted, trench-coat pædo-philes either. We are talking about keen young men and women with a bright future, who underestimate the over-powering force of their own sexuality. They underestimate the deceitfulness of their own hearts. Or they underestimate the predatory wiles of a teenager.

Our churches and youth groups provide the necessary kindling. And as the old fellowship favourite once assured us, "It only takes a spark...". The glow of physical attraction is a nice fire to warm yourself by, but you get burnt when you get too close. The trick is to throw water on it rather than petrol.

The Bible warns us about the dangers. 23,000 Israelites fell in the desert in one day because of their sexual immorality. The details are recorded for our benefit, as a warning (1 Cor 10:8). There is no room in God's church (1 Cor 5:9-12) or in God's heaven (1 Cor 6:9-10) for people who claim to be Christian and continue in sexual immorality.

The Bible sounds this warning to all Christians, especially those who have become complacent (1 Cor 10:12). Yet we somehow think our loftiest leaders are immune to such temptations. Ever since King David, we have had painful reminders that this is simply not true. In fact, leadership opens up new opportunities for the devil to ensnare us (1 Tim 3:6-7).

Fuel for the fire
There a number of reasons why youth leaders are especially vulnerable.

1. The nature of leadership
When you hold a position of responsibility, people trust you. Most parents assume that churches appoint leaders that are utterly reliable. Each time you take young people on an outing, parents express that trust in you.

Few will raise eye-brows when you drop members of the opposite sex home or do some heavy counselling into the night. This means that you will have access to *situations* others don't have access to.

2. The nature of the Bible
The Bible addresses our lives in the most intimate and personal way. Young people often confuse their response to God's word with their response to those who teach them. They may leave a Bible study or talk feeling that the speaker understands their inner life in a special and profound way. After all, we make it our business to address issues like sexuality, decision making, relationships and self-esteem.

This means that you will have access to *feelings* that others don't have access to.

3. The nature of young people

Depending on the age group, most youth groups cover the period of life when teenagers are at their most vivacious and physically attractive. At the same time they are at their most emotionally naive and personally insecure.

The combination is potent. The idea of mature, married men with crushes on 15 year old schoolgirls may sound sick, but it happens. Some surprising names have found their way onto the pencil cases of 15 year olds.

4. The poverty of our churches

Most churches see youth ministry as compulsory even when they lack the leadership resources to staff such work. As a result, young people with any kind of potential are too often pushed prematurely into leadership roles. Without experience, training and supervision, they must face the full range of pressures and temptations that youth ministry generates.

The art of throwing water

The Bible's standard for brother-sister relationships is clear. We are to treat each other "with absolute purity" (1 Tim 5:1–2). When we don't, trouble is just around the corner.

It's for this reason that there have long been some home-spun conventions or safeguards. These were never meant to be a new pharisaic code or moral strait-jacket, but wise advice drawn from painful mistakes. They sound a little old-fashioned, but our grandparents didn't live in a hormone-free world—so it shouldn't surprise us if they can teach us a thing or two. Let's state them in their most extreme form:

- All your conduct should not only *be* above board, but *be seen* to be above board.
- Never be alone with a member of the opposite sex behind a closed door.
- Any counselling should be done by a member of the same sex.

- Dress modestly.
- Discourage the practice of indiscriminate hugging.

Rules like these help, as do church or denominational proto-
cols, but they are no cure for the real problem.

We have to cure ourselves of the feeling that 'it could
never happen to me'. We should have a healthy mistrust of
ourselves—remember, the Bible teaches that the human heart
is deceitful above all else (Jer 17:9).

We have to overcome the isolation that characterizes much
ministry. It's an isolation that is not necessarily cured by 'team'
ministry. Fear of disapproval and intimidation by peers often
prevent us from facing up to the things that drive us—things
that drive us both to new heights of achievement and new
depths of despair. We need to draw near to God and cast our
cares on the one who loved us enough to send his Son into the
world to redeem us. And we need to draw near to at least one
close Christian friend with whom we can frankly share our
deepest struggles.

Above all we need to agree with God. We need to reflect
on what the Bible teaches until we are clear about what God
wants us to do with the wonderful gift of sexuality. Only then
will we see the Bible's 'restrictions' as God's kind guidance of
us (see the 'Read the Bible' section on p. 110).

Cold lives in need of warmth

There is a lot at stake. We live in an age where advertisements
and TV shows imply that everyone is having sex from their
early teens. Videos depicting all kinds of distorted sexuality
are readily available to young kids. The result is wider confusion and insecurity.

There is a great opportunity for Christian leaders to teach
this generation what true love really is. Our youth groups can
be places where a real alternative is offered to the world of
greed, lust, selfishness and destruction. They can be places
relatively free of the pressure to measure up, pair up, make

out and break up. They can be places marked by acceptance, warmth, affection and love. The brother-sister relationship that the Bible envisages is something more beautiful and enduring than many teenagers can imagine.

The apostle Paul saw modelling as the most worthwhile of all careers. He held himself out as a model of Christ-likeness to follow (1 Cor 11:1; Phil 3:17, 4:9). He urges his understudy, Timothy, to do the same (1 Tim 4:11-16).

Teenagers today don't have too many places where they can see the purity of brother-sister love lived out. There aren't many blockbuster movies that have this theme. Three minute music video clips don't seem to have much time for it either. For young, impressionable teenagers to witness this kind of purity and commitment modelled in our lives and taught in our groups, is a profound contribution to make to their lives.

Of course, we not only need to model proper sexual behaviour as leaders but teach the teenagers in our groups to be loving towards one another in this area.

Teaching sex and sexuality to teenagers

The 'sex talk' is an annual event in many youth group teaching programmes. You might get a doctor in to give the talk, or a married couple, or lead it yourself. But we want to suggest that you teach about sex more than once a year.

And that's not just because it looms so large in the world of teenagers. Let me explain why.

The great danger with any teaching that has a strong moral element is that young people will be left with the impression that you are simply saying "Don't". Of course, that is an essential part of what you will be teaching, but it isn't the half of it. The Bible's teaching about sex and sexuality is much wider and deeper than a simple moral command. If we give the impression that we only talk about sex very rarely, and then only in order to say "Don't", then we will not have equipped our young people very well to deal with the tempting and confusing sexual climate they find themselves in.

We can't go into the whole of the Bible's teaching on sexuality here (read *Pure Sex* by Philip Jensen and Tony Payne for
a fuller account),[1] but these brief indications should be enough
to show that it is unhelpful to pigeonhole sexual teaching
into a once-a-year event. Our sexuality determines a huge
part of our behaviour, personality and motivation for acting.
It's therefore both appropriate and biblical that we should
integrate our teaching on sexuality with a teaching plan that
covers the whole counsel of God.

And of course, if we are consistently showing how God's
commands to avoid fornication, adultery and impure thoughts
have good biblical and theological reasons behind them, then
your group will be more likely to resist the pressures on them
to conform to their world, give in to the devil, or succumb
to their raging hormones. And the Bible's reasons are, in the
end, so much more compelling than those expounded by the
moralistic 'no' lobby. Being open, honest and clear, without
obsessively dwelling on the issue, will pay dividends in young
lives that remain untainted by mistakes in this most damaging
of areas.

Two other areas need brief comment.

Homosexuality

It's worth making a brief mention too of what has tradition-
ally been a taboo subject among Christians. If you're a youth
leader for any length of time, it's likely that you will also come
across boys or girls (or leaders) who are tempted with homo-
sexual thoughts. You need to be prepared to work out how to
handle this, to counsel them biblically, and to give them the
right kind of encouragement.[2] It is worthwhile discussing the
question with your minister, and developing a policy on how
to handle the question as and when it arrives.

---

1. Available from Matthias Media.
2. *What Some of You Were* (Matthias Media) is a helpful resource on this topic.

The Mating Game

There is also a need for you to take the initiative about what is deemed acceptable in the group as regards dating and sexual behaviour. For this, you need to enlist the help of the more mature Christians in the group.

Many groups have been ruined by couples who are insepa-rable—you know the ones: they sit at the back of the meet-ings holding hands, and take every opportunity to slip away to be on their own. Likewise, the frantic dating-and-breaking cycles that some groups seem to go through can be damaging to the health of the group. A friendly word with people is often enough: "John, I don't think it's helpful that you cuddle Joanna in front of everyone else—how do you think it makes the girls feel who aren't paired off with anyone else?" "Lizzie, when you come to the group, your aim should be to love and encourage everyone, not just Bob. Try to keep your dating time separate from the group time. It's simply a matter of being loving, and considerate."

Similarly, words of caution to keep relationships quiet and low profile will add greatly to the sense of group togetherness, rather than the envy, jealousy and gossip that can rule when people are pairing off. In fact, it is often more constructive to encourage 'group dating' to be the norm, and for people not to make the exclusive 'going out' commitment—or at least, if they do, to impress upon them the need to work harder at spending time with others from the group.

It's all part of teaching your group to think of others before themselves; in other words, to become like Christ.

Read the Bible

Read the following passages and consider what they have to say:

1. 1 Thessalonians 4:1-8

    • What is "God's will" in this passage?

    • List the reasons Paul gives for obeying God.

2. Matthew 5:27-30

    • What is the sexual sin Jesus has in mind?

    • How seriously does he take it?

3. 1 Corinthians 5:1-5

    • What action does Paul advocate in dealing with this situation?

4. 1 Corinthians 6:9-20

- What hope is there for the sexually immoral?

- What is unique about sexual sin?

What about your group?

1. Review your current practice on teaching about sex—what changes do you need to make?

2. What biblical passages or principles would you apply to a group whose main preoccupation is 'who broke up with whom and why?'.

Matthias Media is an evangelical publishing ministry that seeks to persuade all Christians of the truth of God's purposes in Jesus Christ as revealed in the Bible, and equip them with high-quality resources, so that by the work of the Holy Spirit they will:

- abandon their lives to the honour and service of Christ in daily holiness and decision-making
- pray constantly in Christ's name for the fruitfulness and growth of his gospel
- speak the Bible's life-changing word whenever and however they can—in the home, in the world and in the fellowship of his people.

It was in 1988 that we first started pursuing this mission, and in God's kindness we now have more than 300 different ministry resources being used all over the world. These resources range from Bible studies and books through to training courses and audio sermons.

To find out more about our large range of very useful resources, and to access samples and free downloads, visit our website:

www.matthiasmedia.com.au

How to buy our resources

1. Direct from us over the internet:
   – in the US: www.matthiasmedia.com
   – in Australia and the rest of the world:
     www.matthiasmedia.com.au

2. Direct from us by phone:
   – in the US: 1 866 407 4530
   – in Australia: 1800 814 360 (Sydney: 9663 1478)
   – international: +61-2-9663-1478

Register at our website for our **free** regular email update to receive information about the latest new resources, **exclusive special offers,** and free articles to help you grow in your Christian life and ministry.

3. Through a range of outlets in various parts of the world. Visit www.**matthiasmedia.com.au/information/contact-us** for details about recommended retailers in your part of the world, including www.thegoodbook.co.uk in the United Kingdom.

4. Trade enquiries can be addressed to:
   – in the US and Canada: sales@matthiasmedia.com
   – in Australia and the rest of the world: sales@matthiasmedia.com.au